# Navy SEAL-Proof Your Home

*The Definitive Expert Strategies for Unbreakable Security and Peace of Mind*

## Rocky Becker

# TABLE OF CONTENTS

# CHAPTER 1

# INTRODUCTION TO HOME SECURITY AND RESILIENCE

## Understanding the Importance of Home Security

Home security is paramount in a world where unpredictability is the only certainty. This aspect of daily life often goes unnoticed until a threat emerges, casting light on its critical importance. A robust security system serves as both a deterrent and a shield, offering not only physical protection but also the invaluable gift of peace of mind. Understanding the significance of home security necessitates a consideration of its multifaceted nature, encompassing physical barriers, technological advancements, and psychological preparedness.

The physical structure of a home forms the first line of defense against external threats. The design and materials used in constructing doors, windows, and walls play a vital role in this regard. Solid core doors, reinforced frames, and impact-resistant glass are essential components that can withstand attempts at forced entry. Beyond construction materials, the strategic placement of barriers like fences and gates can provide an additional layer of security, creating a buffer zone that delays and deters intruders. The goal is to transform the home into a fortress where unauthorized entry is as challenging as possible.

However, physical barriers alone are insufficient in ensuring comprehensive security. Technological advancements offer significant enhancements, turning traditional homes into smart fortresses. The integration of surveillance cameras, motion detectors, and alarm systems adds an additional layer of vigilance. Modern security systems can be programmed to send alerts directly to homeowners' smartphones, ensuring that one remains informed of any disturbances even when away from home. The mere presence of visible security cameras can deter potential intruders, while hidden cameras provide a means of capturing evidence without alerting the perpetrator. Moreover, smart locks and biometric entry systems eliminate the vulnerabilities associated with traditional keys, allowing access only to those authorized.

The importance of home security extends beyond the tangible; it encompasses an emotional and psychological dimension. A secure home is a sanctuary where one can retreat from the chaos of the outside world. It is a place where families gather, memories are made, and lives are lived without the looming fear of intrusion. The psychological impact of knowing that one's home is secure cannot be overstated. It fosters a sense of control in an unpredictable world, reducing anxiety and enabling individuals to focus on other aspects of their lives.

Understanding the importance of home security involves recognizing the potential threats that necessitate such measures. While the likelihood of encountering a home invasion may seem remote, the consequences of such an event are severe enough to warrant proactive measures. Home security is also about safeguarding against lesser-known threats, such as environmental hazards. Implementing measures to detect smoke, carbon monoxide, and gas leaks can prevent disasters before they occur, protecting both property and lives.

In addition to physical security and technological tools, resilience is integral to a comprehensive home security strategy. Resilience involves preparing for the unforeseen and being equipped to adapt to new challenges. It is about having contingency plans in place, such as backup power systems for essential electronics in case of power outages. Resilience also involves maintaining a supply of essential items, such as food, water, and medications, to sustain the household in emergencies. In this way, a secure home becomes not only a line of defense but also a hub of self-sufficiency.

The importance of home security extends to fostering a culture of awareness and vigilance among all household members. It is crucial that everyone understands the security protocols in place and knows how to respond in the event of an emergency. Regular drills and discussions can ensure that these procedures become second nature, minimizing panic and confusion when faced with a real threat.

Communication plays a pivotal role in maintaining a secure environment. Establishing reliable lines of communication with neighbors and local authorities can enhance security efforts. A cooperative community is more likely to deter criminal activity, as neighbors can look out for one another and report suspicious behavior.

In the broader context, home security is part of a larger framework of personal safety and community resilience. It requires continuous evaluation and adaptation to keep pace with evolving threats. The landscape of risk is constantly changing, driven by technological advancements and societal shifts. As such, a static approach to home security is insufficient. Homeowners must be proactive in staying informed about new security technologies, methods of intrusion, and effective countermeasures.

Understanding the importance of home security is not merely about protecting physical property; it is about safeguarding the intangible aspects of life. It is about ensuring that one's home remains a haven of safety and comfort. In a world where uncertainty abounds, investing in home security is an investment in peace of mind, allowing individuals to live without fear and focus on what truly matters.

# Lessons from Navy SEAL Tactics

Navy SEALs, renowned for their expertise in executing complex missions, offer a treasure trove of insights applicable to home security and resilience. These elite operatives undergo rigorous training to master not only physical endurance but also mental fortitude and strategic thinking. By adapting their principles and tactics, homeowners can create a robust defense system, transforming their living spaces into well-protected sanctuaries.

One of the fundamental tenets of Navy SEAL training is situational awareness. This involves a heightened sensitivity to one's environment, constantly assessing potential threats and changes. At home, this means being attuned to the surroundings, knowing the neighborhood, and recognizing unusual activity. Simple actions, such as regularly inspecting the perimeter of the property or noting unfamiliar vehicles, can go a long way in preventing threats. The practice of staying alert and aware is pivotal, allowing homeowners to preemptively address vulnerabilities before they are exploited.

SEALs are also trained in the art of deception and misdirection, skills that can be surprisingly effective in home security. By creating an illusion of enhanced security, such as prominently displaying security system signage or installing dummy cameras, potential intruders may be deterred. This tactic is about projecting strength and preparedness, making the home appear a less attractive target. The concept of "layered security" is another SEAL-inspired strategy. Just as SEALs use multiple defense mechanisms to safeguard their missions, a layered approach to home security involves implementing various measures that work together to form a cohesive defense network. This could include a combination of physical barriers, surveillance systems, and alarm responses. Each layer serves as a backup to the others, ensuring that if one measure fails, others are in place to compensate.

Another lesson from SEAL training is the importance of adaptability. SEALs operate in ever-changing environments, requiring them to adjust their strategies on the fly. Homeowners can mirror this adaptability by staying informed about new technologies and security trends, continuously updating their security measures to counter evolving threats. Regularly evaluating and upgrading security systems ensures that the home remains protected against emerging risks.

Communication is a cornerstone of SEAL operations. They rely on seamless coordination and information sharing to execute missions successfully. For homeowners, establishing clear communication channels within the household and with trusted neighbors can significantly enhance security. Families should have predefined plans for various scenarios, ensuring that everyone knows their role and how to respond in an emergency. Engaging with neighbors through community watch programs or informal agreements to look out for each other's properties can foster a supportive network that bolsters individual security efforts.

Physical fitness and mental resilience are critical components of SEAL preparation, underscoring the need for homeowners to be prepared for unexpected situations. While physical fitness may not seem directly related to home security, it plays a role in emergency preparedness. Being physically capable of responding quickly to threats, whether through escaping danger or assisting family members, is invaluable. Mental resilience, on the other hand, equips individuals to remain calm and collected under pressure, enabling them to make rational decisions during crises. Homeowners can cultivate mental resilience by practicing stress-reduction techniques and engaging in exercises that simulate emergency scenarios.

Redundancy is another principle SEALs adhere to, ensuring that they have backup systems in place for every critical operation. In the context of home security, this translates to having contingency plans. For instance, if an intruder disables the primary alarm system, a secondary system or manual alert mechanism should be available. Similarly, having backup power sources, such as generators or battery packs, can maintain essential security functions during power outages. Redundancy extends to personal safety plans as well, with alternative escape routes and meeting points designated in case the primary plan is compromised.

The ability to improvise and innovate is a hallmark of SEAL tactics. Homeowners can apply this by thinking creatively about security solutions. This might involve using everyday items to reinforce entry points or devising unique ways to conceal valuables. Encouraging a mindset of innovation can lead to the development of personalized security measures that address specific vulnerabilities unique to the home.

Finally, SEALs are taught the value of debriefing and learning from each mission, a practice that can be adapted for home security. After any security incident or drill, homeowners should conduct a thorough review of what transpired, identifying strengths and areas for improvement. This reflective process allows for continuous learning and adaptation, ensuring that the home's security measures evolve alongside potential threats.

By incorporating these lessons from Navy SEAL tactics, homeowners can build a comprehensive security strategy that is proactive, adaptable, and resilient. The goal is to create an environment where the risks are minimized, and the household remains prepared to face any challenge that may arise. This approach not only protects physical assets but also fosters a sense of confidence and peace of mind, knowing that the home is a well-fortified refuge.

# The Concept of Bugging In vs. Bugging Out

When faced with the prospect of an emergency or crisis, one of the most pivotal decisions you'll need to make is whether to "bug in" or "bug out." This choice hinges on a variety of factors, including the nature of the threat, your location, and the resources available to you. Understanding the nuances of both options is essential for developing a comprehensive home security and resilience plan that can effectively safeguard you and your loved ones.

Bugging in refers to the strategy of staying put in your home during a crisis. This approach leverages the familiar environment and resources of your household, transforming it into a stronghold against external threats. The decision to bug in is often based on the belief that your home is sufficiently fortified and stocked to withstand the specific challenges posed by the crisis. This could be anything from a natural disaster like a blizzard or hurricane to a civil disturbance or pandemic.

The advantages of bugging in are numerous. Your home provides a level of comfort and familiarity that is difficult to replicate elsewhere. It houses your stockpile of supplies, including food, water, medical necessities, and other essentials that are critical during an emergency. Additionally, remaining in place allows you to maintain control over your immediate environment, reducing the risks associated with evacuation, such as exposure to hazards or becoming stranded without resources.

However, the effectiveness of bugging in relies heavily on preparation. Your home must be adequately fortified to withstand potential threats, both natural and human-made. This means ensuring that entry points are secure, windows are reinforced, and security systems are operational. Stockpiling is equally important, requiring a well-rounded collection of supplies that can sustain your household for an extended period. This includes non-perishable food items, potable water, hygiene products, and necessary medications. Energy independence, through means such as solar panels or generators, can also be crucial if the crisis disrupts local utilities.

The alternative, bugging out, involves leaving your home and relocating to a safer location. This decision is typically made when staying put poses a greater risk than leaving. Factors that might necessitate bugging out include the threat of structural damage to your home, a mandatory evacuation order, or a situation where remaining in place becomes untenable due to a lack of resources or escalating danger.

Bugging out requires a different set of preparations. A bug-out plan should include predetermined routes and destinations, such as a family member's home in a safer area or a designated shelter. It's vital to have a bug-out bag ready at all times, packed with essential items for survival on the move. This bag typically contains a portable supply of food and water, clothing suitable for the climate, first aid supplies, personal identification, and any necessary tools or equipment for navigation and self-sufficiency.

The decision to bug out should be made with careful consideration of timing and circumstances. Leaving too early may expose you to unnecessary risks, while delaying evacuation could trap you in a dangerous situation. Communication plays a critical role here; staying informed through reliable news sources and local alerts can provide the information needed to make an informed decision.

Both bugging in and bugging out have their inherent challenges and risks. For instance, while bugging in offers the comfort of home, it can also lead to isolation if communication and power lines are disrupted. Conversely, bugging out may offer safety from immediate dangers but could involve navigating chaotic environments and dealing with logistical challenges, like finding shelter or fuel.

Collaboration and planning with family members or trusted neighbors can significantly enhance the effectiveness of either strategy. Establishing a network of contacts ensures that you have support and can share resources or information if needed. This communal approach can be particularly beneficial when bugging in, as it allows for mutual assistance in securing homes and sharing supplies.

Ultimately, the choice between bugging in and bugging out should be guided by a clear understanding of the situation and a realistic assessment of your preparedness. Flexibility is key—being able to adapt your plan in response to changing conditions can make all the difference. Regularly reviewing and updating your emergency plans ensures that they remain relevant and effective, providing peace of mind that you are ready to face whatever challenges arise.

## Assessing Potential Threats

Understanding the potential threats that could compromise your home's security is a crucial aspect of fortifying your living space. Recognizing these threats requires a comprehensive approach that encompasses both common and unexpected scenarios. By systematically assessing these vulnerabilities, you can tailor your security measures to effectively mitigate risks and enhance your home's resilience.

The first step in assessing potential threats is to conduct a thorough evaluation of your home's immediate environment. Begin by examining the neighborhood and its crime statistics. Local law enforcement agencies often provide reports that highlight trends in residential burglaries, vandalism, and other crimes. Understanding these patterns allows you to identify the specific risks prevalent in your area, such as high rates of break-ins or instances of vehicle theft.

Beyond crime, environmental factors pose their own set of threats. Natural disasters, such as floods, earthquakes, hurricanes, and wildfires, can severely impact your home's security and safety. Assessing your location's susceptibility to these events is vital. For instance, homes in flood-prone areas should prioritize flood defenses, while those in regions prone to wildfires must focus on creating defensible space around the property. Evaluating historical data on natural disasters in your area can provide valuable insights into potential risks.

Your home's structural vulnerabilities also warrant attention. Weak points such as poorly maintained doors, windows, and roofs can be exploited by both human intruders and environmental forces. Conducting a physical examination of the property's exterior and interior can reveal areas that require reinforcement. This might involve upgrading locks, reinforcing window glass, or addressing structural issues that could be exacerbated by severe weather.

Technological threats are increasingly relevant in today's interconnected world. The rise of smart home devices has introduced new vulnerabilities that can be exploited by cybercriminals. Assessing your home's digital security is as critical as its physical security. Ensure that your Wi-Fi network is protected with strong passwords and encryption, and regularly update the firmware on all connected devices to address potential security flaws. Being vigilant about phishing attacks and avoiding suspicious links can also help safeguard your home from digital intrusions.

Personal circumstances can influence the types of threats you may face. For example, individuals with high public profiles or those involved in contentious professions may attract unwanted attention. If this applies to you, consider implementing additional security measures such as surveillance systems and personal alarms. Understanding your unique situation allows you to tailor your security strategy accordingly.

Assessing potential threats also involves anticipating future risks. The threat landscape is constantly evolving, driven by technological advancements, societal changes, and global events. Staying informed about emerging threats, such as new burglary techniques or advancements in cybercrime, is crucial for adapting your security measures. Subscribing to security newsletters, attending community safety meetings, and engaging with online forums dedicated to home security can provide valuable updates and insights.

Once you have identified the potential threats to your home, the next step is to prioritize them based on their likelihood and potential impact. This prioritization process guides the allocation of resources, ensuring that the most pressing risks are addressed first. For instance, if your neighborhood experiences frequent home invasions, investing in robust door and window security should be a top priority. Conversely, if your area is prone to power outages, ensuring backup power sources may take precedence.

Collaboration with local authorities and neighbors can enhance your threat assessment efforts. Law enforcement agencies can offer guidance on crime prevention measures, while community watch programs provide an additional layer of security through collective vigilance. Engaging with neighbors to share information about suspicious activity or recent incidents fosters a sense of community and strengthens your overall security strategy.

## Setting Goals for Home Fortification

Establishing clear and attainable goals is a cornerstone of effective home fortification. By setting these objectives, you can systematically enhance your home's security, ensuring it becomes a bastion of safety for you and your loved ones. This process involves identifying priorities, understanding the unique needs of your household, and implementing practical measures to address potential vulnerabilities.

To begin, it is essential to assess the current state of your home's security. Take a comprehensive inventory of existing measures, such as locks, lighting, and surveillance systems. Evaluate their effectiveness and identify areas in need of improvement. This initial assessment provides a baseline from which you can develop a structured plan. Consider the unique characteristics of your property, including its size, layout, and location. Each home presents distinct challenges and opportunities for fortification, and your goals should reflect this individuality.

Once you've assessed the current state of your security, prioritize your goals based on potential risks and available resources. Some objectives may require immediate attention due to pressing threats, such as a recent increase in neighborhood crime. Others may be more long-term, focusing on building resilience against unlikely but severe events like natural disasters. By categorizing goals into short-term, medium-term, and long-term, you can allocate resources efficiently and maintain focus on achieving them over time.

Short-term goals often involve quick, impactful changes that bolster security with minimal effort and cost. These might include replacing outdated locks with more robust alternatives, installing motion-sensor lights around the perimeter, or trimming overgrown shrubs that could serve as hiding spots for intruders. Such measures provide an immediate boost to home security and serve as a foundation for more comprehensive strategies.

Medium-term goals require a bit more investment in terms of time and resources but offer substantial improvements to your home's security. Consider upgrading to a smart security system that integrates cameras, alarms, and remote monitoring capabilities. This not only enhances protection but also adds a layer of convenience, allowing you to monitor your home from anywhere. Additionally, reinforcing entry points with stronger doors and windows or installing a sturdy fence around the property can significantly deter potential intruders.

Long-term goals focus on fortifying your home against less frequent but potentially devastating events. Developing a comprehensive disaster preparedness plan is a prime example. This involves creating an emergency kit, establishing evacuation routes, and ensuring that your home is equipped to withstand natural disasters common to your area, such as earthquakes or floods. Investing in off-grid energy solutions, such as solar panels or backup generators, can also be part of a long-term strategy to maintain security and self-sufficiency during power outages.

Throughout the goal-setting process, consider the specific needs and circumstances of your household. Families with young children may prioritize goals that focus on safety and accessibility, such as installing childproof locks or creating safe play areas. Those with elderly members might emphasize measures that facilitate quick evacuation or medical response. Tailoring your goals to fit your household's dynamics ensures that everyone feels secure and protected.

Communication is key when setting goals for home fortification. Involve all members of your household in the process, fostering a sense of shared responsibility and collaboration. Discuss potential threats and brainstorm solutions together, ensuring that everyone's concerns are addressed. This collaborative approach not only strengthens security but also builds a collective awareness that enhances overall readiness.

As you work toward achieving your goals, remain flexible and open to adapting your strategies. The landscape of threats is ever-evolving, and your security measures should be dynamic enough to respond to new challenges. Regularly review and adjust your goals to reflect changes in your environment, technological advancements, and lessons learned from past experiences. This iterative process ensures that your home remains a well-fortified sanctuary, capable of withstanding a wide range of potential threats.

Documenting your progress is an important part of the goal-setting journey. Maintain a record of completed tasks, ongoing projects, and future plans. This documentation not only serves as a reminder of your achievements but also provides valuable insights for future reference. In the event of a security breach or emergency, having a detailed record of your fortification efforts can aid in troubleshooting and recovery.

# CHAPTER 2

# CONDUCTING A COMPREHENSIVE SECURITY AUDIT

## Identifying Vulnerabilities

Conducting a comprehensive security audit of your home is a fundamental step toward ensuring its safety and resilience. This process involves a meticulous examination of your property to identify any vulnerabilities that could be exploited by intruders or compromised during emergencies. By systematically assessing your home's defenses, you can effectively address weaknesses and implement strategies to bolster security.

Begin the audit by inspecting the exterior of your home, as it serves as the first line of defense against potential threats. Walk around the perimeter and take note of any areas that may be vulnerable to unauthorized access. Pay particular attention to doors and windows, as these are common entry points for burglars. Ensure that all doors are equipped with high-quality deadbolts and strike plates. Consider reinforcing door frames with metal plates to prevent them from being kicked in. For windows, check that they are fitted with locks and, if applicable, consider adding security film to make the glass more resistant to breaking.

Lighting is another crucial aspect of exterior security. Adequate lighting can deter intruders by eliminating hiding spots and increasing the likelihood of detection. Evaluate the current lighting setup around your property, including entryways, pathways, and driveways. Install motion-activated lights to cover blind spots and areas with limited visibility. Solar-powered options can be a cost-effective and environmentally friendly solution for illuminating your property. Additionally, consider integrating smart lighting systems that can be controlled remotely, allowing you to simulate occupancy when you are away.

Fencing and landscaping also play a role in your home's security profile. Inspect fences for any signs of damage or deterioration that could be exploited. Ensure that gates have sturdy locks and consider using thorny or dense plants along the fence line to further deter intruders. Avoid landscaping features that provide cover for potential trespassers, such as tall shrubs or trees near windows. Instead, opt for low-maintenance, security-friendly landscaping that maintains clear sightlines around your property.

Once the exterior audit is complete, turn your attention to the interior. Begin by evaluating the strength and functionality of locks on all doors and windows. Consider upgrading to smart locks that offer enhanced security features, such as keyless entry and activity tracking. These locks can be especially useful for households with multiple occupants, as they provide a convenient way to manage access without the need for physical keys.

Security systems are a critical component of interior protection. Assess the current system in place, if any, and determine whether it meets your security needs. A comprehensive security system should include door and window sensors, motion detectors, and surveillance cameras. Modern systems often offer remote monitoring capabilities, allowing you to receive alerts and view live footage from your smartphone. When installing cameras, ensure they cover key areas such as entry points, hallways, and common spaces. Opt for cameras with night vision capabilities for around-the-clock protection.

In addition to traditional security measures, consider potential environmental threats that could impact your home. Smoke detectors, carbon monoxide alarms, and water leak sensors are essential devices for safeguarding against domestic hazards. Test these devices regularly to ensure they are functioning correctly and replace batteries as needed. If you live in an area prone to natural disasters, such as earthquakes or hurricanes, evaluate the structural integrity of your home and make necessary reinforcements to withstand such events.

The audit should also address digital security, particularly if you have a smart home with interconnected devices. Secure your Wi-Fi network by using strong, unique passwords and enabling encryption protocols. Regularly update the firmware on all smart devices to protect against vulnerabilities and hacks. Be cautious with the information you share online, as oversharing can inadvertently reveal details about your security setup or absence from home.

Personal habits and routines can unintentionally create security vulnerabilities. Analyze daily routines to identify potential risks, such as leaving doors unlocked or failing to arm the security system when leaving the house. Encourage all household members to adhere to security protocols, ensuring that everyone is vigilant and conscientious about maintaining a secure environment.

## Evaluating Current Security Measures

Evaluating the effectiveness of your current security measures is an integral part of conducting a comprehensive security audit. This evaluation not only highlights the strengths and weaknesses of your existing setup but also guides future enhancements to ensure a robust defense system tailored to your specific needs. To achieve this, a detailed assessment of both physical and digital security measures is essential, providing a well-rounded perspective on your home's safety.

The process begins with scrutinizing the physical barriers that protect your home. Doors and windows, as primary entry points, deserve particular attention. Examine their condition, focusing on the durability of materials and the quality of locks. Are your doors solid-core, equipped with deadbolts, and reinforced with strike plates? If you find any inadequacies, consider upgrading to more secure options, such as steel-reinforced doors or high-security locks. Windows should also be fitted with robust locks, and where possible, reinforced with security film to prevent easy breakage. Additionally, consider using window bars or grilles for added protection, particularly for ground-floor windows.

Lighting plays a crucial role in deterring potential intruders, as well-lit properties are less attractive targets. Assess the current lighting around your home, especially at entry points and along pathways. Are there dark areas that could provide cover for someone attempting to breach your security? Motion-activated lights are an effective solution for illuminating these areas, making it difficult for intruders to approach undetected. For a more sustainable option, solar-powered lights offer an eco-friendly alternative that requires minimal maintenance.

Surveillance systems are another key component of home security, providing both a deterrent and a means of documenting activity around your property. Evaluate the placement and quality of your security cameras, ensuring they cover critical areas such as doors, driveways, and backyards. High-definition cameras with night vision capabilities are ideal, allowing for clear footage regardless of lighting conditions. Consider upgrading to a system that offers remote access, enabling you to monitor your home from anywhere via a smartphone or computer.

Alarm systems are a staple of home security, alerting you and authorities to potential breaches. If your home is equipped with an alarm system, test its functionality regularly to ensure it is responsive and effective. Check that all sensors, whether on doors, windows, or motion detectors, are operational and properly placed. If your system is outdated, upgrading to a modern version with smart technology features can provide enhanced security through real-time alerts and remote management.

Digital security is increasingly important in today's interconnected world, where smart home devices are common. Begin by assessing the security of your Wi-Fi network, as it serves as the backbone of your digital infrastructure. Use strong, unique passwords and enable encryption to protect against unauthorized access. Regularly update the firmware on all connected devices, such as smart locks, cameras, and thermostats, to mitigate vulnerabilities that hackers could exploit. Additionally, be wary of phishing scams and suspicious links that could compromise your network security.

Beyond physical and digital measures, evaluate the human element of your security strategy. This involves assessing the awareness and preparedness of household members in maintaining safety protocols. Are all family members familiar with the operation of security systems and emergency procedures? Conduct regular drills to reinforce these practices, ensuring everyone knows how to respond effectively in the event of an emergency. Encourage a culture of vigilance, where household members are mindful of locking doors and windows, setting alarms, and reporting suspicious activity.

Security measures should also be evaluated in the context of your local environment. Consider the specific risks associated with your neighborhood, such as high crime rates or susceptibility to natural disasters. Tailor your security strategy to address these local factors, ensuring that your home is resilient to the challenges it faces. Engaging with community watch programs or local law enforcement can provide additional insights and resources for enhancing security.

# Creating a Detailed Security Checklist

Creating a detailed security checklist is a crucial step in conducting a comprehensive security audit of your home. This checklist serves as a structured guide, ensuring that no aspect of your home's security is overlooked. It acts as both a diagnostic tool and a roadmap for improvement, helping you systematically assess and enhance the safety of your living environment.

To begin crafting your security checklist, start with the perimeter of your property. This includes fences, gates, and any other barriers that define the boundary of your home. Verify that fences are intact and free of damage that could allow unauthorized entry. Ensure that gates are equipped with reliable locks and that there are no gaps or weak points that could be exploited. Consider adding signage, such as "Beware of Dog" or "Property Under Surveillance," to deter potential intruders.

Next, evaluate the lighting around your property. Proper illumination is essential for both safety and security, as it reduces hiding spots and increases visibility. Check that all outdoor lights are functional and positioned to cover key areas such as driveways, pathways, and entry points. Motion-sensor lights are particularly effective, as they activate when movement is detected, alerting you to potential intruders while conserving energy. Solar-powered options offer a sustainable solution for areas where electrical wiring may be impractical.

Doors and windows are primary entry points and should be a focal point of your checklist. Inspect all exterior doors, ensuring they are constructed of solid materials and equipped with deadbolts. Reinforce door frames with metal plates to prevent them from being kicked in. For added security, consider installing peepholes or video doorbells to monitor who is at the door without opening it. Windows should be fitted with sturdy locks and, where applicable, reinforced with security film to deter break-ins. For ground-level windows, consider installing window bars or grilles.

Your home's interior security measures should also be meticulously examined. Start with your alarm system, if you have one. Test all sensors, including door and window contacts, motion detectors, and glass break sensors, to ensure they are operational and correctly placed. If your system is outdated, upgrading to a modern, smart system with remote monitoring capabilities can enhance security and provide peace of mind. Smoke detectors, carbon monoxide alarms, and fire extinguishers are also critical components of interior safety. Verify that these devices are functioning properly and replace batteries as needed.

Surveillance systems offer both deterrence and documentation of suspicious activity. Assess the placement and quality of your cameras, ensuring they capture clear footage of all critical areas, such as entrances, driveways, and backyards. Cameras with night vision capabilities are particularly valuable for round-the-clock monitoring. If feasible, consider integrating your cameras with a smart home system that allows remote access and real-time alerts.

Digital security is an increasingly important aspect of home protection, especially with the prevalence of smart devices. Start by securing your Wi-Fi network with a strong, unique password and enabling encryption to prevent unauthorized access. Regularly update the firmware on all connected devices, such as smart locks, cameras, and thermostats, to address potential vulnerabilities. Be cautious with the information shared online, as oversharing can inadvertently reveal details about your security setup or absence from home.

Landscaping can significantly impact your home's security profile. Inspect the layout of your yard, ensuring that trees, shrubs, and other vegetation do not provide cover for potential intruders. Trim back overgrown plants, particularly near windows and doors, to maintain clear sightlines around your property. Consider using thorny or dense plants to create natural barriers that deter unauthorized access.

Include emergency preparedness in your checklist. This involves creating and maintaining an emergency kit, establishing evacuation routes, and developing a communication plan for household members in the event of a crisis. Regularly review and update these plans to ensure they remain effective and relevant.

# Prioritizing Improvements

When conducting a security audit, prioritizing improvements is a critical step in enhancing your home's safety. This process involves evaluating identified vulnerabilities and determining which enhancements will provide the most significant increase in security. By systematically prioritizing these improvements, you ensure that resources are allocated effectively, addressing the most pressing risks first and creating a safer living environment.

Start by reviewing the results of your security audit, focusing on areas that pose the greatest threat to your home. Consider the likelihood of each vulnerability being exploited and the potential impact on your safety and peace of mind. For instance, if your neighborhood has experienced a recent surge in break-ins, bolstering entry points such as doors and windows should be a top priority. In contrast, if your home is located in an area prone to power outages, investing in backup power solutions may take precedence.

Once you have identified high-priority vulnerabilities, develop a plan to address them. This plan should outline specific actions to be taken, estimated costs, and a timeline for completion. Short-term improvements often involve relatively quick and inexpensive fixes, such as upgrading locks or installing additional lighting. These enhancements provide an immediate boost to security and serve as a foundation for more comprehensive measures.

Medium-term improvements may require more substantial investments of time and resources but offer significant benefits. Consider installing a modern security system with features such as remote monitoring, motion detection, and real-time alerts. This not only enhances protection but also adds convenience, allowing you to manage your home's security from anywhere. Additionally, reinforcing entry points with stronger doors and windows or installing a sturdy fence around your property can deter potential intruders.

For long-term improvements, focus on fortifying your home against less frequent but severe threats. Developing a comprehensive disaster preparedness plan is an example of a long-term strategy. This involves creating an emergency kit, establishing evacuation routes, and ensuring that your home is equipped to withstand natural disasters common to your area, such as earthquakes or floods. Investing in off-grid energy solutions, like solar panels or backup generators, can also be part of a long-term strategy to maintain security and self-sufficiency during power outages.

Throughout the prioritization process, consider the specific needs and circumstances of your household. Families with young children may prioritize goals that focus on safety and accessibility, such as installing childproof locks or creating safe play areas. Those with elderly members might emphasize measures that facilitate quick evacuation or medical response. Tailoring your goals to fit your household's dynamics ensures that everyone feels secure and protected.

Communication is key when prioritizing improvements. Involve all members of your household in the process, fostering a sense of shared responsibility and collaboration. Discuss potential threats and brainstorm solutions together, ensuring that everyone's concerns are addressed. This collaborative approach not only strengthens security but also builds a collective awareness that enhances overall readiness.

As you work toward achieving your priorities, remain flexible and open to adapting your strategies. The landscape of threats is ever-evolving, and your security measures should be dynamic enough to respond to new challenges. Regularly review and adjust your priorities to reflect changes in your environment, technological advancements, and lessons learned from past experiences. This iterative process ensures that your home remains a well-fortified sanctuary, capable of withstanding a wide range of potential threats.

## Documenting Your Security Plan

Documenting your security plan is a crucial step in conducting a comprehensive security audit. It serves as a detailed record of your current security measures, identified vulnerabilities, and the strategies you intend to implement to enhance your home's safety. A well-documented plan not only guides your efforts but also provides a valuable resource for everyone in the household, ensuring consistency and clarity in your approach to security.

Begin by creating an overview of your property's layout, including a detailed map that highlights key areas such as entry points, vulnerable spots, and existing security features. This visual representation helps you and other household members understand the current security landscape, making it easier to identify areas that require attention. Include notations for doors, windows, gates, fences, and any other structures that contribute to your home's security perimeter.

Next, compile a comprehensive list of all existing security measures currently in place. This inventory should cover both physical and digital aspects, including locks, lighting, alarm systems, surveillance cameras, and digital security protocols like Wi-Fi encryption. For each measure, note its condition, effectiveness, and any maintenance or upgrades needed. This documentation provides a clear picture of your starting point and helps prioritize future improvements.

Identify and record any vulnerabilities discovered during your security audit. Be thorough in your assessment, considering factors such as outdated equipment, lack of coverage, and potential human errors in security practices. Categorize these vulnerabilities based on their severity and the likelihood of exploitation. This prioritization allows you to focus on addressing the most critical issues first, ensuring that resources are used efficiently to enhance overall security.

Develop a detailed action plan to address the vulnerabilities identified. For each issue, outline the steps needed to mitigate risks, including any equipment purchases, installations, or changes in procedures. Assign responsibilities to household members for specific tasks, ensuring that everyone is involved and accountable. Establish a timeline for each action item, setting realistic deadlines to maintain momentum and track progress.

Incorporate a section in your documentation dedicated to emergency preparedness. This includes creating and maintaining an emergency kit, establishing evacuation routes, and developing a communication plan for household members in the event of a crisis. Regularly review and update these plans to ensure they remain effective and relevant, adapting to any changes in your household or environment.

Include a checklist of routine security maintenance tasks in your documentation. This checklist should cover regular testing and upkeep of security systems, such as alarm sensors, camera functionality, and digital security updates. Establish a schedule for these tasks, ensuring they are performed consistently to maintain the effectiveness of your security measures.

Engage all household members in the documentation process, encouraging their input and feedback. This collaborative approach fosters a sense of shared responsibility and ensures that everyone understands their role in maintaining a secure environment. Conduct regular meetings to discuss progress, address concerns, and update the plan as needed. This ongoing dialogue helps build a culture of vigilance and readiness within your household.

Store your documented security plan in a secure but accessible location, ensuring that all household members know where to find it. Consider keeping both a physical copy and a digital version for added convenience and security. In the event of a security breach or emergency, having this documentation readily available can aid in troubleshooting and recovery efforts.

# CHAPTER 3

# FORTIFYING ENTRY POINTS

## Reinforcing Doors and Windows

Securing the entry points of your home, particularly doors and windows, is a fundamental aspect of fortifying your residence against potential intrusions. As the primary barriers between the inside of your home and the outside world, these access points require robust reinforcement to deter unauthorized entry and safeguard your household. Understanding how to effectively reinforce doors and windows involves a combination of strategic upgrades, material enhancements, and the implementation of advanced security technologies.

Begin with the doors, which are often the first target for intruders seeking access. A solid core door, made from materials such as wood, steel, or fiberglass, provides a formidable barrier compared to hollow-core doors, which are more susceptible to forced entry. If your current doors are hollow-core, consider replacing them with more durable options. Additionally, ensure that the door frames are strong and well-secured; reinforcing the frame with metal strike plates can significantly increase resistance to forced entry.

The locking mechanism is critical in securing doors. High-quality deadbolts should be installed on all exterior doors. Choose a deadbolt with a minimum one-inch throw bolt to provide adequate security. Ensure that the strike plate is secured with screws that penetrate deep into the door frame, ideally reaching the studs. Consider upgrading to a smart lock system, which offers keyless entry and the ability to monitor and control access remotely. This not only enhances security but also provides convenience and peace of mind.

Adding a door reinforcement kit can provide an extra layer of protection. These kits typically include door jamb reinforcement, hinge shields, and additional strike plates, all designed to withstand attempts to force the door open. Peepholes or video doorbells are also valuable additions, allowing you to identify visitors before opening the door, which adds another layer of security.

Sliding glass doors present unique challenges due to their large glass panels. To reinforce these doors, install a security bar or rod in the track to prevent them from being forced open. Anti-lift devices can also be installed to prevent the door from being removed from its track. Consider applying shatterproof film to the glass, which holds the glass together even if it is broken, making it more difficult for an intruder to gain entry.

Windows, while often overlooked, are another common entry point for burglars. Reinforcing them begins with the locks; ensure that all windows have functional, secure locks. For added security, consider installing pin locks or keyed locks, which are more difficult to tamper with. Window security film is an effective deterrent, as it strengthens the glass and makes it shatter-resistant. In the event of an attempted break-in, the film holds the glass together, delaying entry and increasing the likelihood of detection.

For ground-level windows, consider installing window bars or grilles. These provide a physical barrier that deters entry without compromising visibility or ventilation. If window bars are not aesthetically desirable, consider installing decorative grilles that enhance both security and curb appeal. Ensure that any security bars installed are equipped with quick-release mechanisms, allowing for easy egress in the event of an emergency.

Casement windows, which open outward, can be secured with heavy-duty locks and locking pins that prevent the window from being pried open. Double-hung windows can be reinforced with sash locks and additional security pins that restrict movement. For added security, install sensors that alert you when a window is opened, providing real-time notifications of potential intrusions.

Incorporating technology into your window security strategy can significantly enhance protection. Install glass break sensors that trigger an alarm if a window is shattered. These sensors are particularly useful for windows that are not easily visible or accessible from the main living areas. Consider integrating these sensors into a broader security system that includes cameras and motion detectors for comprehensive coverage.

While reinforcing doors and windows, it is essential to maintain a balance between security and aesthetics. Choose reinforcement options that complement the architectural style of your home, ensuring that security enhancements do not detract from its appearance. Many modern security products are designed with aesthetics in mind, offering sleek, unobtrusive solutions that blend seamlessly with your home's design.

Regular maintenance and inspection of doors and windows are critical to ensuring their continued effectiveness. Check for signs of wear, such as rusted locks, warped frames, or deteriorated weather stripping, and address these issues promptly. Routine maintenance not only preserves the integrity of your security measures but also extends the lifespan of your doors and windows.

# Installing Advanced Locking Systems

Securing your home with advanced locking systems is an essential component of fortifying entry points. As technology continues to evolve, so do the methods used by intruders to gain access to homes. To counteract these threats, investing in state-of-the-art locking systems offers enhanced protection and peace of mind. Whether you are upgrading existing locks or installing new ones, understanding the features and benefits of advanced locking systems is crucial for making informed decisions that enhance your home's security.

Traditional locks, while still widely used, often lack the sophistication needed to deter determined intruders. Advanced locking systems, however, incorporate modern technology to provide a robust defense against unauthorized access. One popular option is the smart lock, which offers keyless entry through methods such as biometric recognition, smartphone apps, or keypads. This eliminates the need for physical keys, reducing the risk of lost or stolen keys being used to gain entry. Smart locks also offer the convenience of managing access remotely, allowing you to lock and unlock doors from anywhere with an internet connection.

Biometric locks, which use fingerprint or facial recognition, provide a high level of security by ensuring that only authorized individuals can enter. These locks are particularly useful for households with multiple occupants, as they can store numerous profiles and grant access to each member. The precision of biometric technology minimizes the risk of unauthorized access, as it relies on unique personal identifiers that are difficult to replicate.

Keypad locks are another advanced option, offering the ability to set unique access codes for each user. This feature is especially beneficial for granting temporary access to guests, service providers, or house sitters without having to distribute physical keys. Keypad locks often include features such as auto-locking and tamper alarms, adding an extra layer of security.

For those seeking maximum security, consider installing interconnected lock systems that integrate with your home security system. These systems offer seamless connectivity between locks, alarms, and surveillance cameras, providing comprehensive protection and real-time alerts in the event of a security breach. Integration with smart home devices allows for automation and enhanced control over your security environment, such as setting locks to engage automatically when the alarm is armed or when you leave the house.

When selecting an advanced locking system, consider the compatibility with your existing doors and the ease of installation. Many smart locks are designed to retrofit standard deadbolts, making them a convenient choice for upgrading security without extensive modifications. Additionally, evaluate the power source of the lock, whether it is battery-operated or hardwired, and ensure that it aligns with your preferences and needs. Regular maintenance, such as replacing batteries or updating firmware, is essential to maintain the functionality and security of these systems.

While advanced locking systems offer numerous benefits, it is important to complement them with other security measures for a holistic approach. Reinforcing door frames, installing security cameras, and using additional deterrents such as signs or lights can enhance the effectiveness of your locking system. Furthermore, consider the placement of locks and ensure that all entry points, including garages and secondary doors, are equipped with appropriate security measures.

Educating household members on the proper use and management of advanced locking systems is crucial for maintaining security. Ensure that everyone understands how to operate the locks, manage access codes, and respond to alerts or notifications. Encourage regular review and updating of access codes to mitigate the risk of compromised security, especially after changes in household members or service providers.

## Utilizing Security Bars and Grilles

Securing entry points with security bars and grilles is an effective strategy for enhancing home protection. These physical barriers serve as a formidable deterrent to potential intruders, providing an additional layer of security that complements other measures like advanced locks and alarm systems. While often associated with a more traditional approach to security, modern security bars and grilles have evolved in design and functionality, offering both robust protection and aesthetic appeal.

The first step in utilizing security bars and grilles is to assess the specific needs of your home. Consider the layout of your property, the location of vulnerable entry points, and the level of security required. Ground-floor windows, basement access points, and sliding glass doors are common targets for intruders, making them prime candidates for the installation of bars or grilles. These barriers are particularly beneficial in areas with higher crime rates, providing peace of mind and a visible deterrent to potential break-ins.

When selecting security bars, it is important to choose options that balance strength with visual appeal. Heavy-duty steel bars are a popular choice due to their durability and resistance to tampering. They can be custom-fitted to your windows and doors, ensuring a snug fit that maximizes security. To enhance aesthetics, many manufacturers offer bars with decorative designs that complement the architectural style of your home. This allows you to maintain curb appeal while reinforcing security.

For those who prefer a less obtrusive look, transparent security grilles are an excellent alternative. Made from materials like polycarbonate or reinforced glass, these grilles provide the same level of protection without obstructing views or natural light. They are ideal for preserving the aesthetic integrity of your home while still offering a high level of security. Additionally, retractable grilles can be installed, allowing you to open and close them as needed, providing flexibility in appearance and function.

Installation of security bars and grilles should be approached with care, ensuring that they are securely mounted and capable of withstanding force. Professional installation is recommended to guarantee that all components are properly fitted and anchored. This is particularly important for grilles on doors, which must be able to withstand attempts to pry them open. Ensure that all installations comply with local building codes and safety regulations, particularly for windows that may serve as emergency exits.

While security bars and grilles are effective in deterring intruders, it is crucial to prioritize safety and accessibility. Install quick-release mechanisms on bars and grilles covering windows that are designated emergency escape routes. These mechanisms allow for rapid removal in case of a fire or other emergencies, ensuring that household members can exit safely. Educate everyone in the household on how to operate these releases, conducting regular drills to reinforce their use.

Maintenance of security bars and grilles is essential to ensure their longevity and effectiveness. Regularly inspect them for signs of wear or damage, such as rust or loose fittings, and address these issues promptly. Clean and lubricate moving parts of retractable grilles to maintain smooth operation. By keeping these barriers in optimal condition, you ensure that they continue to provide reliable protection.

Incorporating security bars and grilles into your overall home security strategy requires a thoughtful approach. Consider their integration with other security measures, such as surveillance cameras or motion-sensor lighting, to create a comprehensive defense system. The presence of bars and grilles can enhance the effectiveness of these technologies by providing additional physical barriers that slow down intruders, increasing the likelihood of detection and response.

# Incorporating Smart Technology

Incorporating smart technology into your home security system is a transformative way to fortify entry points and enhance overall protection. As technology rapidly advances, smart home devices have become more accessible and user-friendly, offering innovative solutions to bolster security without compromising convenience or aesthetics. By integrating these smart technologies, you can create a robust, interconnected security network that not only protects your home but also adapts to your lifestyle.

Smart locks are one of the most effective ways to secure entry points while embracing modern technology. These devices allow you to control access to your home without traditional keys, using methods such as smartphone apps, keypads, or biometric recognition. With smart locks, you can monitor and manage access remotely, granting entry to family members or service providers with ease. Features like auto-locking and real-time notifications ensure that your doors are always secure, providing peace of mind whether you're at home or away.

Another essential component of smart security is the integration of video doorbells. These devices enable you to see and communicate with visitors at your door, even when you're not home.

Equipped with high-definition cameras and motion sensors, video doorbells provide real-time alerts and video feeds, allowing you to monitor activity and deter potential intruders. Many models also include night vision and two-way audio, enhancing your ability to interact with visitors and identify suspicious behavior.

Smart cameras are a versatile addition to any home security system, offering comprehensive surveillance of entry points and surrounding areas. These cameras can be strategically placed to cover blind spots and provide continuous monitoring, recording footage that can be accessed remotely. Advanced features such as motion detection, facial recognition, and integration with other smart devices allow for a seamless security experience. By connecting smart cameras to a central hub or app, you can receive instant alerts and take immediate action if a security breach is detected.

Incorporating smart lighting is another effective strategy for fortifying entry points. Smart lights can be programmed to turn on automatically at specific times or in response to motion, creating the illusion of occupancy even when you're not home. This deters potential intruders by suggesting that someone is present, reducing the likelihood of a break-in. Additionally, smart lights can be controlled remotely, allowing you to adjust settings and monitor activity from anywhere.

Integrating a smart home hub is a valuable way to synchronize all your security devices and create a cohesive system. A central hub connects and controls various smart technologies, enabling them to communicate and work together efficiently. Through a single app or interface, you can manage locks, cameras, lights, and other devices, streamlining your security efforts and enhancing responsiveness. This interconnected approach not only simplifies security management but also maximizes the effectiveness of each device.

Voice-activated assistants, such as Amazon Alexa or Google Assistant, can further enhance your smart security system. These devices allow you to control and monitor your security features using voice commands, providing a hands-free solution that integrates seamlessly with your daily routine. By linking your voice assistant to your smart home hub, you can easily lock doors, adjust lighting, or view camera feeds with simple vocal prompts.

When incorporating smart technology into your security strategy, it's essential to prioritize cybersecurity. Protect your devices with strong, unique passwords and enable encryption where possible. Regularly update firmware and software to ensure that your security devices remain protected against vulnerabilities and potential cyber threats. Consider setting up a separate network for smart devices to further enhance security and prevent unauthorized access.

# Enhancing Garage and Basement Security

The garage and basement are often overlooked when it comes to home security, yet they represent some of the most vulnerable entry points. Enhancing security in these areas is crucial for a comprehensive defense strategy. With a few targeted measures, you can significantly reduce the risk of unauthorized entry and protect both your property and loved ones.

Garages, particularly those attached to the main house, serve as a direct access point for intruders. Begin by assessing the garage door, which is often the largest and most visible entry. Ensure that it is made of sturdy material and equipped with a reliable locking mechanism. If the garage door operates electronically, consider upgrading to a model with rolling code technology. This technology changes the access code every time the remote is used, preventing code grabbing by potential intruders.

Manual garage doors should be secured with additional locks, such as slide bolts or padlocks, to reinforce security. If the door includes windows, cover them with frosted film or blinds to obscure the view of valuables inside. For further protection, install a door sensor or alarm that alerts you if the garage door is opened unexpectedly.

The door connecting the garage to the house is another critical point of entry. Treat this door with the same level of security as your front door. Install a solid core door with a high-quality deadbolt lock. Consider adding a peephole or smart lock for added convenience and security. Regularly check the door frame and hinges for signs of wear and reinforce them as needed.

Lighting plays a vital role in deterring intruders, particularly around the garage area. Install motion-activated lights near the garage door and other entry points, ensuring they cover all angles. Well-lit areas are less attractive to potential intruders, as they increase the risk of detection. Solar-powered lights offer an energy-efficient option to keep these areas illuminated without a significant increase in electricity usage.

Basements, often secluded and less visible, require specific security considerations. Start by reinforcing basement windows, which tend to be smaller and easier for intruders to access. Install security bars or grilles on windows to provide a physical barrier, and consider using shatterproof film to prevent the glass from being easily broken. Ensure that all window locks are functional and secure; upgrade them if necessary to provide additional protection.

Basement doors should be as robust as all other exterior doors. Equip them with sturdy locks and reinforce the door frame to withstand attempts at forced entry. A deadbolt lock is essential for added security, and the door should fit snugly within its frame to prevent being easily pried open. Consider installing a door sensor or alarm to alert you if the door is tampered with or opened unexpectedly.

Investing in a security system that includes the garage and basement is a practical step in enhancing overall security. Cameras installed in these areas can monitor activity and provide real-time alerts in the event of a breach. Select weather-resistant models for outdoor use and consider those with night vision capabilities to ensure round-the-clock surveillance. Integration with a smart home system allows you to access camera feeds remotely, providing peace of mind even when you're away.

Organizing and minimizing clutter in the garage and basement can also contribute to security. A tidy space makes it easier to spot unusual activity or signs of tampering. Store tools and ladders securely, as these can be used by intruders to gain access to higher entry points. Consider using lockable storage units for valuables or sensitive items, adding an extra layer of security within these spaces.

Educating household members about the importance of securing the garage and basement is essential. Encourage everyone to regularly check that doors and windows are locked, especially during nighttime or when the house is unoccupied. Establish a routine for securing entry points and involve all family members in the process to ensure consistency and vigilance.

# CHAPTER 4

# SETTING UP SURVEILLANCE SYSTEMS

## Choosing the Right Cameras and Sensors

Selecting the right cameras and sensors for your home surveillance system is a critical step in ensuring comprehensive security coverage. With an array of options available on the market, understanding the features and functionalities of these devices can significantly enhance your ability to monitor and protect your property. By carefully considering factors such as placement, connectivity, and detection capabilities, you can tailor your surveillance system to meet the unique needs of your home.

Begin by evaluating the areas that require monitoring. High-traffic entry points, such as front and back doors, are obvious candidates for camera placement, but consider also covering secondary entryways, driveways, and perimeters. For these locations, outdoor cameras with weather-resistant features are essential. These devices are designed to endure harsh conditions while providing clear, reliable footage. Look for cameras with durable housings and wide operating temperature ranges to ensure they function optimally throughout the year.

Resolution is a key factor in camera selection, as it directly impacts the clarity of the footage. High-definition cameras, with 1080p resolution or higher, capture detailed images that can be crucial in identifying individuals or vehicles. Consider investing in cameras with night vision capabilities to maintain visibility in low-light conditions. Infrared LEDs or thermal imaging sensors enable cameras to capture clear footage even in complete darkness, adding a layer of security during nighttime hours.

The field of view provided by a camera determines how much area it can cover. Wide-angle lenses are beneficial for monitoring large spaces, while narrow lenses are more suited to focused, detailed surveillance. Some cameras offer pan, tilt, and zoom (PTZ) functionalities, allowing you to adjust the view remotely and focus on specific areas as needed. This versatility can be particularly useful for monitoring expansive outdoor areas or following moving objects.

Connectivity options should also be considered when selecting cameras. Wired cameras offer stable, uninterrupted connections, making them ideal for areas where consistent monitoring is crucial. However, wireless cameras provide flexibility in placement and are easier to install, as they eliminate the need for extensive cabling. Many modern wireless cameras connect via Wi-Fi and can be integrated into your home network, allowing for remote access and control through mobile apps.

Integration with other smart home devices is another important consideration. Cameras that can connect with smart home hubs or voice assistants allow for seamless operation and control. This integration enables features such as automated recording when motion is detected or voice-activated camera feeds, enhancing the overall effectiveness of your surveillance system.

In addition to cameras, incorporating sensors into your surveillance setup can provide an additional layer of security. Motion sensors are particularly effective in detecting movement within a designated area, triggering alarms or cameras to start recording. Look for sensors with adjustable sensitivity settings to minimize false alarms from pets or environmental factors. Some advanced motion sensors include features like thermal detection, which distinguishes between humans and animals, reducing unnecessary alerts.

Door and window sensors are also valuable components of a comprehensive surveillance system. These devices alert you when a door or window is opened unexpectedly, providing immediate notifications that can prevent unauthorized access. Many sensors are designed to integrate with security systems, triggering alarms or sending alerts to your smartphone for real-time response.

Environmental sensors, such as those detecting smoke, carbon monoxide, or water leaks, can further enhance home security by addressing potential hazards. By connecting these sensors to your surveillance system, you ensure that your home is monitored not only for intrusions but also for safety threats. This holistic approach to security provides peace of mind, knowing that all aspects of your home are protected.

When setting up a surveillance system, consider the importance of storage and data management. Cameras with local storage options, such as SD cards, provide a straightforward solution for recording footage. However, cloud storage offers a more secure and accessible option, allowing you to access footage from anywhere and providing backup in case of device damage or theft. Evaluate the storage needs based on the number of cameras, resolution, and recording frequency to select a suitable plan.

Privacy is a crucial consideration when installing surveillance systems. Ensure that your cameras and sensors do not inadvertently capture footage of neighboring properties or public spaces. Familiarize yourself with local regulations regarding surveillance to ensure compliance and avoid potential legal issues. Communicate with neighbors about your surveillance setup, fostering transparency and cooperation within the community.

## Strategic Placement for Maximum Coverage

Strategic placement of surveillance systems is pivotal to ensuring maximum coverage and protection of your property. The effectiveness of cameras and sensors is largely dependent on their positioning, which can mean the difference between comprehensive monitoring and leaving blind spots for potential intruders to exploit. With thoughtful planning and execution, you can establish a surveillance network that is both efficient and unobtrusive, providing peace of mind and security.

Understanding the layout and vulnerabilities of your property is the first step in determining the best locations for surveillance equipment. Start by conducting a thorough assessment of your home's exterior and interior, identifying high-risk areas and potential entry points. Commonly targeted spots include front and back doors, ground floor windows, driveways, and garages. These should be prioritized when planning your surveillance strategy.

Outdoor cameras should be positioned to cover the perimeter and main access points. Placing cameras at a height that is difficult to tamper with is crucial, generally around 9 to 10 feet off the ground. This height provides a comprehensive view while protecting the camera from vandalism. Utilizing wide-angle lenses can help cover larger areas, reducing the number of cameras needed for effective surveillance. However, ensure that cameras are angled downward slightly to capture faces and movement more clearly.

Driveways and walkways benefit from surveillance placement that captures the full length of these paths. Position cameras to monitor vehicles entering and exiting the property, focusing on license plates and facial recognition. For longer driveways, consider additional cameras at strategic intervals to ensure complete coverage. Motion-activated lights can complement these setups, illuminating areas and enhancing camera footage clarity during nighttime hours.

The front door is a critical surveillance point, as it is the most common entry for both welcome guests and potential intruders. A doorbell camera provides a direct view of anyone approaching the entrance, with the added benefit of two-way audio for real-time communication. Pairing doorbell cameras with additional cameras focused on the front yard or porch can provide context and capture a broader view of activities in this area.

Backyards and side entrances often require discreet yet effective monitoring. Cameras positioned here should cover secondary doors, patios, and yards. Consider using wireless cameras for these areas to avoid the need for extensive wiring, allowing for flexible placement. Ensure these cameras are weatherproof and equipped with night vision to maintain continuous surveillance regardless of environmental conditions.

For interior coverage, focus on areas where intruders are likely to pass through or search. Hallways, staircases, and common rooms are ideal for indoor cameras. Positioning cameras at entrances to these areas can capture clear images of anyone moving through the home. In rooms with valuable items, consider placing cameras that focus on safes, electronics, or other high-value possessions.

Sensors play a complementary role in maximizing coverage. Motion sensors should be strategically placed to cover entry points and corridors, triggering alerts or recording when movement is detected. Adjust the sensitivity of these sensors to avoid false alarms from pets or environmental factors. Door and window sensors provide an additional layer of security by notifying you of any unexpected openings.

The integration of cameras and sensors with a central system or app allows for streamlined management and monitoring. Choose a system that provides remote access, enabling you to view camera feeds and receive notifications in real time. This connectivity ensures that you are always aware of activities around your property, even when you are not physically present.

While achieving comprehensive coverage, it is essential to respect privacy and comply with local regulations. Avoid positioning cameras in areas that infringe on the privacy of neighbors or capture footage beyond your property lines. Familiarize yourself with applicable laws regarding surveillance to ensure compliance and prevent legal complications.

# Integrating Surveillance with Home Automation

Integrating surveillance with home automation represents a significant leap in enhancing security systems. This convergence of technology not only boosts the efficacy of your surveillance setup but also offers unprecedented convenience, turning your home into a smart, responsive environment. By marrying these two systems, you create a cohesive network that reacts dynamically to various situations, providing comprehensive security coverage while simplifying the management of your home.

The heart of integrating surveillance with home automation lies in the smart home hub. This central unit acts as the command center, connecting and coordinating various devices, including cameras, sensors, lights, and alarms. By linking these elements, your home becomes an interconnected ecosystem, capable of executing complex commands based on specific triggers or schedules. Choosing a hub that supports multiple protocols, such as Zigbee, Z-Wave, or Wi-Fi, ensures compatibility with a wide range of devices, allowing for flexibility and scalability as your needs evolve.

Surveillance cameras integrated into this system offer more than just passive monitoring. With automation, these cameras can be programmed to respond to specific events. For instance, when a motion sensor detects activity at the front door, the system can automatically activate the camera, record footage, and notify you via a smartphone app. This immediate alert system allows for real-time response, whether you're at home or miles away.

Advanced features like facial recognition can be incorporated to further enhance security. Cameras with this capability can differentiate between familiar faces and strangers, customizing alerts accordingly. If an unknown face is detected, the system might trigger additional security measures, such as turning on exterior lights or activating an alarm. This intelligent approach minimizes false alarms while ensuring that genuine threats are promptly addressed.

Lighting is a powerful tool in home automation, particularly when synchronized with surveillance. Smart lights can be set to turn on automatically in response to detected motion, deterring potential intruders by creating the illusion of occupancy. Furthermore, integrating lights with surveillance allows for improved visibility in camera footage, ensuring that any activity is captured clearly, even in low-light conditions. Automated lighting schedules can also be programmed to mimic regular usage patterns, enhancing security when the home is unoccupied.

Smart locks are another crucial component of automated surveillance systems. These devices can be controlled remotely, allowing you to lock or unlock doors from anywhere, and can be integrated with your surveillance cameras for added security. For example, when a family member approaches the door, facial recognition technology can confirm their identity and automatically unlock the door, streamlining access without compromising safety.

Voice assistants, such as Amazon Alexa or Google Assistant, enrich the integration of surveillance and automation by providing hands-free control. Through voice commands, you can access camera feeds, adjust lighting, or modify security settings, making it easier than ever to manage your home security. This feature is particularly beneficial for individuals with limited mobility or those who prefer a more seamless interaction with their smart home devices.

For a truly integrated experience, consider incorporating environmental sensors into your home automation system. These sensors detect changes in smoke, carbon monoxide, or water levels, and can trigger specific responses to enhance safety. For instance, if a water leak is detected, the system might automatically shut off the water supply and notify you immediately, preventing damage and reducing the risk of costly repairs.

Privacy and cybersecurity are paramount when integrating surveillance with home automation. Ensure that all devices are secured with strong passwords and regularly updated to protect against vulnerabilities. Consider setting up a separate network for your smart home devices to safeguard your primary internet connection and data. Familiarize yourself with the privacy settings of each device, controlling who has access to video feeds and personal information.

## Monitoring and Maintenance Protocols

Effective surveillance systems require diligent monitoring and maintenance protocols to ensure they function optimally and provide the highest level of security. While setting up a surveillance system is a significant step in safeguarding your home, ongoing attention to its operation is essential for long-term efficacy. By establishing a routine for monitoring and maintenance, you can maximize the lifespan and performance of your surveillance equipment, ensuring your home remains well-protected.

Begin by implementing a regular schedule for reviewing footage and system alerts. This practice helps you stay informed about activities around your property and detect any unusual patterns or behaviors. Depending on the level of security needed, you might choose to review footage daily, weekly, or even in response to specific alerts. Many modern systems offer features such as motion detection and smart notifications, which help prioritize important events and reduce the need for constant manual review.

Utilizing cloud storage solutions can simplify the process of organizing and accessing surveillance footage. Cloud services provide secure, remote storage, ensuring that your recordings are safe from damage or theft. They also offer the convenience of accessing footage from anywhere, whether through a smartphone, tablet, or computer. When choosing a cloud storage option, consider factors such as storage capacity, retention periods, and privacy policies to select a service that aligns with your security needs.

Regularly test your surveillance equipment to confirm that all components are functioning correctly. This includes checking cameras for clear image quality, verifying that sensors are responsive, and ensuring that all connections are secure. For wired systems, inspect cables for signs of wear or damage, while wireless systems should be checked for stable connectivity. Replace any faulty equipment promptly to maintain comprehensive coverage and prevent gaps in security.

Keep software and firmware up to date, as manufacturers frequently release updates that address security vulnerabilities and improve functionality. Set up automatic updates if possible, or establish a routine for manually checking and applying updates. Staying current with software enhancements not only protects your system from potential threats but also ensures access to the latest features and improvements.

Battery-operated devices, such as wireless cameras and sensors, require periodic battery replacement to ensure continued operation. Establish a schedule for checking battery levels and replacing them as needed, using high-quality batteries to extend the lifespan of your devices. Consider investing in rechargeable batteries and a charging station for an environmentally friendly and cost-effective solution.

Establish a protocol for responding to system alerts and notifications. This may involve designating specific household members to receive alerts or setting up a chain of command for addressing potential security breaches. Develop a plan for verifying alerts, such as checking live camera feeds or contacting neighbors, and outline steps for contacting authorities if necessary. Clear communication and established procedures help ensure a quick and effective response to any security concerns.

Consider scheduling periodic professional maintenance checks, particularly for complex or large-scale surveillance systems. Professional technicians can conduct thorough inspections, perform advanced troubleshooting, and provide expert recommendations for optimizing system performance. These regular check-ups can identify potential issues before they become significant problems, preserving the integrity and reliability of your surveillance network.

# Legal and Ethical Considerations

Establishing a surveillance system at home involves more than just technical setup; it requires careful consideration of legal and ethical dimensions. These considerations are critical to ensuring that your surveillance efforts are not only effective but also compliant with laws and respectful of privacy.

Understanding these aspects helps you navigate the complex landscape of surveillance while maintaining trust and harmony within your community.

The legal framework governing surveillance varies widely by jurisdiction, making it imperative to familiarize yourself with local laws before installing any equipment. In many places, laws stipulate where cameras can be placed, what they can record, and how that footage can be used. For instance, it is often illegal to record audio without consent, which can affect the placement and usage of certain surveillance devices. Consulting with legal professionals or local authorities can provide clarity on applicable regulations, helping you avoid potential legal pitfalls.

One of the primary legal considerations involves the expectation of privacy. Individuals have a reasonable expectation of privacy in certain areas, such as inside their homes or private spaces like bathrooms and changing rooms. When setting up cameras, it is crucial to ensure that they do not inadvertently capture footage of these areas. Additionally, avoid positioning cameras in a way that invades the privacy of neighbors, such as pointing them directly into adjacent yards or windows. Violations of privacy expectations can result in legal actions and damage relationships with neighbors.

Ethical considerations are equally important in the realm of surveillance. Installing cameras brings with it the responsibility to use them judiciously and respectfully. Consider the impact of surveillance on those who live in or visit your home. Open communication about the presence and purpose of cameras fosters transparency and mutual understanding. Informing household members and regular visitors about surveillance measures can alleviate concerns and demonstrate your commitment to respecting their privacy.

Consent is a cornerstone of ethical surveillance. Whenever possible, obtain consent from those who might be recorded, particularly in shared living spaces. This practice not only aligns with ethical standards but can also serve as a protective measure against potential legal challenges. In situations where obtaining consent is not feasible, such as monitoring public-facing areas like driveways or sidewalks, signage indicating the presence of surveillance can serve as a notice, reducing the likelihood of disputes.

Data protection and security are integral to both legal compliance and ethical responsibility. Surveillance systems often collect sensitive information that must be stored securely to prevent unauthorized access. Implement robust data protection measures, such as encryption and access controls, to safeguard footage. Regularly update passwords and restrict access to authorized individuals only. In the event of a data breach, having a response plan in place can mitigate damage and demonstrate your commitment to protecting personal information.

Retention policies for surveillance footage are another critical aspect of data management. Determine how long footage will be stored and under what circumstances it will be deleted or retained. Laws may dictate specific retention periods, so it is essential to align your policies with legal requirements. Additionally, consider ethical implications, such as the potential for misuse if footage is kept indefinitely. By establishing clear and transparent retention policies, you enhance trust and accountability.

Transparency extends beyond those directly affected by surveillance. Consider engaging with your broader community about your surveillance practices. This could involve participating in neighborhood meetings or forums to discuss the role of surveillance in community safety. Open dialogue can help address concerns, dispel misconceptions, and foster a sense of shared responsibility for security.

Balancing security with respect for privacy is a nuanced challenge, requiring vigilance and adaptability. As technology evolves, so too do the legal and ethical standards that govern its use. Staying informed about changes in laws and best practices is essential for maintaining a responsible surveillance system. Engage with professional organizations, attend workshops, or subscribe to relevant publications to keep abreast of developments in the field.

# CHAPTER 5

# CREATING SAFE ROOMS AND SECURE ZONES

## Designing an Impenetrable Safe Room

Designing an impenetrable safe room is a critical endeavor for those seeking to ensure maximum security during emergencies. A well-planned safe room can provide refuge during natural disasters, home invasions, or other threats, offering peace of mind and a tangible line of defense. The process of creating such a room involves careful consideration of location, construction materials, access control, and essential supplies. By thoughtfully addressing each of these elements, you can construct a space that not only protects but also sustains occupants until help arrives.

Selecting the location for your safe room is the first crucial step. Ideally, it should be easily accessible from the main living areas of your home, allowing you to reach it quickly in a crisis. Basements often serve as excellent safe room locations due to their natural insulation from external threats like severe weather or intruders. However, if a basement is not feasible, consider a central room on the ground floor with minimal windows and exterior walls, as these features increase vulnerability to breaches.

Building materials are fundamental in ensuring the resilience of your safe room. Reinforced concrete is a popular choice due to its strength and durability, offering protection against both brute force and natural disasters. Steel is another viable option, providing robust defense against forced entry and ballistic threats. For those constructing a safe room within an existing structure, using steel plates or rebar-reinforced walls can enhance the room's integrity without requiring complete reconstruction. Additionally, ensure that the ceiling is fortified, as this is often an overlooked point of entry for potential threats.

The door to your safe room is a critical component, as it serves as the primary barrier to entry. Invest in a high-quality, solid-core door equipped with a heavy-duty deadbolt lock. Consider upgrading to a steel security door with multiple locking points for enhanced protection. The door should open inward to prevent blockages from outside debris or forced entry attempts. Additionally, installing a peephole or external camera can allow occupants to assess the situation outside the room without compromising their safety.

Ventilation is essential in a safe room to ensure a continuous supply of fresh air. A dedicated air filtration system can protect against airborne contaminants, such as smoke or chemical agents, while maintaining a comfortable environment. Ensure that the system is discreetly installed to prevent external tampering and regularly serviced to maintain optimal performance.

Communication is another vital aspect of a functional safe room. Equip the room with a reliable means of contacting the outside world, such as a landline phone or an emergency radio. Mobile phones are convenient, but they should not be relied upon exclusively due to potential network outages during emergencies. Consider installing a two-way radio system for direct communication with emergency services or family members outside the home.

Stocking your safe room with essential supplies ensures that occupants can remain secure and comfortable for an extended period if necessary. Water is a top priority, with at least one gallon per person per day recommended for drinking and sanitation. Non-perishable food items, such as canned goods and energy bars, should also be stored, providing sustenance for several days. Include a comprehensive first aid kit, along with any necessary medications, to address potential injuries or health concerns.

Lighting is crucial for maintaining visibility and morale within the safe room. Battery-operated lanterns or flashlights are ideal, as they function independently of the main power supply. Keep an ample supply of batteries on hand to ensure continuous illumination. Additionally, consider installing a manual or battery-powered light switch to control lighting without relying on external electricity.

Comfort items, such as blankets, pillows, and basic toiletries, can significantly improve the experience of staying in a safe room for prolonged periods. These items help preserve a sense of normalcy and well-being, reducing stress and anxiety during high-pressure situations.

Regular drills and practice sessions are essential for ensuring that all household members are familiar with the safe room's location and operation. Establishing a clear plan for reaching the room quickly and efficiently can save valuable time during an emergency. Conduct periodic reviews of the room's supplies and functionality, making necessary adjustments based on changing needs or circumstances.

## Stocking Your Safe Room with Essentials

Stocking your safe room with essentials is a critical step in ensuring that you are well-prepared for emergencies, be they natural disasters, home invasions, or other unforeseen events. A well-stocked safe room serves not only as a refuge but as a self-sustaining environment capable of supporting you and your loved ones until it is safe to emerge or help arrives. Careful selection and organization of supplies can make all the difference in comfort and survival during a crisis.

Water is the most crucial element to consider when stocking your safe room. The general recommendation is to store at least one gallon of water per person per day, with a minimum supply for three to five days. This amount accounts for both drinking and basic hygiene. Consider purchasing commercially bottled water or using food-grade water storage containers. For longer-term emergencies, a water filtration system or purification tablets can be invaluable, ensuring access to safe drinking water should your primary supply run low.

Food supplies should focus on non-perishable items that require minimal preparation. Canned goods, dried fruits, nuts, and energy bars are excellent choices due to their long shelf life and nutritional value. Include a manual can opener to ensure access to canned foods. Freeze-dried meals are another option, especially when paired with a portable camping stove for heating. When selecting food supplies, consider dietary restrictions and preferences to maintain morale and health during extended stays.

A comprehensive first aid kit is indispensable in a safe room, providing the means to address minor injuries and medical needs until professional help is available. Your kit should include adhesive bandages, sterile gauze, antiseptic wipes, tweezers, scissors, adhesive tape, and pain relievers. Additionally, stock any prescription medications required by household members, ensuring a supply sufficient for at least a week. Familiarize yourself with the contents of the kit, and consider taking a basic first aid and CPR course to enhance your preparedness.

Lighting is essential for maintaining visibility and psychological comfort within the safe room. Battery-operated lanterns and flashlights are reliable sources of light that operate independently of the main power supply. Store an ample supply of batteries to ensure continuous operation. Solar-powered or hand-crank flashlights offer additional options, reducing reliance on disposable batteries.

Consider installing a battery-powered LED light strip for ambient lighting, which can be more energy-efficient and longer-lasting.

Communication devices are vital for staying informed and reaching out for assistance during emergencies. A landline phone, if available, provides a stable connection unaffected by power outages. Mobile phones are convenient but should be supplemented with a portable charger or power bank to maintain functionality. An emergency radio, particularly one with NOAA (National Oceanic and Atmospheric Administration) capabilities, can keep you updated on weather conditions, emergency broadcasts, and other critical information.

Comfort items, while often overlooked, can significantly enhance the livability of a safe room during prolonged stays. Blankets, sleeping bags, and pillows provide warmth and rest, essential for maintaining energy and morale. Basic toiletries, such as toilet paper, toothpaste, and wet wipes, contribute to personal hygiene and comfort. A change of clothes, including sturdy footwear, can be beneficial if you need to leave the safe room in adverse conditions.

Tools and materials for basic repairs or adjustments should also be included. A multi-tool or a small toolkit with essentials like screwdrivers, pliers, and duct tape can prove invaluable for addressing minor issues that may arise. Rope or heavy-duty cord can be useful for securing items or even aiding in escape if necessary.

Personal documents and valuables should be stored securely within the safe room. Important papers such as identification, insurance policies, and legal documents should be kept in a waterproof container. Additionally, consider including cash and spare keys for vehicles or secondary properties. These items ensure you have access to necessary resources and information once the emergency has passed.

Finally, consider the mental and emotional well-being of those who may use the safe room. Books, puzzles, or games provide entertainment and distraction, helping to alleviate stress and anxiety. Comforting items, such as family photos or small mementos, can offer reassurance and a sense of normalcy during uncertain times.

# Establishing Perimeter Security Zones

Establishing perimeter security zones forms the first line of defense in safeguarding your property, creating a buffer that deters potential intruders and provides early warning of any breach attempts. These zones are critical in a comprehensive security strategy, as they address vulnerabilities before threats reach your home. By strategically layering defenses and utilizing a combination of physical barriers, surveillance technology, and smart landscaping, you can effectively fortify your perimeter and enhance overall safety.

The outermost perimeter typically comprises fences, walls, or hedges that define the boundary of your property. These barriers serve as both physical and psychological deterrents, signaling to potential intruders that access is restricted. When selecting a boundary material, consider factors such as durability, aesthetics, and local regulations. Chain-link fences, for example, are cost-effective and allow for visibility, while solid walls or privacy fences offer greater concealment and sound reduction. For a natural look, dense hedges or thorny shrubs can provide an eco-friendly barrier that blends seamlessly with the environment.

Gates are integral to perimeter security, controlling access points and facilitating the flow of authorized entry. A robust, lockable gate, whether manual or automated, adds an extra layer of protection. For automated gates, options such as remote controls, keypads, or smartphone integration offer convenience while maintaining security. Ensure that gates are constructed from durable materials and equipped with reliable locking mechanisms to prevent tampering. Adding intercom systems or video doorbells at entry points allows for secure communication with visitors before granting access.

Lighting plays a crucial role in perimeter security, deterring unauthorized entry and improving visibility. Motion-activated lights along the boundary illuminate potential intruders, increasing their exposure and discouraging attempts to breach the perimeter. These lights can be strategically positioned at entry points, near gates, and along pathways to ensure comprehensive coverage. Solar-powered options provide an energy-efficient solution, reducing dependency on the electrical grid.

Surveillance systems, including cameras and motion sensors, enhance perimeter security by providing real-time monitoring and alerts. Cameras placed at strategic points along the perimeter can capture footage of suspicious activity, serving as both a deterrent and a valuable tool for identifying intruders. Modern surveillance systems often include features such as night vision, wide-angle lenses, and remote access, allowing you to monitor the perimeter from anywhere. Integrating these systems with a central security hub enables automated responses, such as triggering alarms or notifying authorities, when a breach is detected.

Landscaping serves as both a deterrent and a means of enhancing perimeter security. Designing the landscape with security in mind can create obstacles that slow down or discourage intruders. Thorny bushes or cacti planted near fences or windows act as natural deterrents, while gravel pathways can alert you to approaching footsteps. Ensure that trees and shrubs are trimmed regularly to eliminate hiding spots for potential intruders and maintain clear sightlines for surveillance cameras.

Signage is a simple yet effective method of reinforcing perimeter security. Clearly visible signs indicating the presence of surveillance cameras, alarm systems, or guard dogs can deter would-be intruders by signaling that the property is actively monitored. Ensure that signs are strategically placed at entry points and along the perimeter to maximize visibility and impact.

Regular maintenance and inspections of the perimeter are essential to ensure that security measures remain effective. Routinely check fences, gates, and locks for signs of wear or damage, and repair or replace any compromised elements promptly. Test lighting and surveillance systems regularly to confirm their functionality and update software and firmware as needed. By staying proactive, you maintain the integrity of your perimeter defenses and address potential vulnerabilities before they can be exploited.

Engaging with neighbors and community watch programs can further enhance perimeter security. A network of vigilant neighbors increases the likelihood of detecting suspicious activity and provides additional eyes on your property when you're away. Sharing information about potential threats or security concerns fosters a sense of community and collective responsibility for safety.

# Planning Emergency Escape Routes

Planning emergency escape routes is a vital aspect of home safety, providing a clear pathway to safety during a crisis. Whether facing a fire, natural disaster, or security threat, having a well-thought-out escape plan can be the difference between life and death. By carefully designing and practicing these routes, you ensure that all household members know how to respond quickly and effectively, minimizing panic and confusion in emergencies.

Begin by assessing the layout of your home to identify potential escape routes. Consider all possible exits, including doors, windows, and any alternative paths that could be used in an emergency. Each room should have at least two exits to provide options if one is blocked or inaccessible. In multi-story homes, ensure that upper floors have escape ladders or other means of descent, allowing occupants to exit safely without relying solely on stairways.

Mapping out these escape routes is a crucial step in the planning process. Create a floor plan of your home, clearly marking each exit and the path leading to it. Highlight primary and secondary routes for each room, ensuring that all household members are familiar with these pathways. Practice using these maps to navigate your home in low-light conditions, simulating situations where visibility may be compromised.

Incorporating technology can enhance the effectiveness of your emergency escape plan. Install smoke and carbon monoxide detectors throughout your home to provide early warning of potential threats. Ensure that these devices are regularly tested and maintained to guarantee their functionality. Consider integrating smart home technology, such as automated lighting systems, which can illuminate escape routes during emergencies, aiding navigation and reducing confusion.

Communication is key to a successful escape plan. Establish a system for alerting household members in the event of an emergency, such as a designated signal or phrase. Practice this communication method during drills to ensure that all individuals respond promptly and efficiently. Additionally, designate a safe meeting point outside the home where everyone can gather once they have evacuated. This location should be far enough from the house to avoid danger but close enough to reach quickly.

Emergency drills are essential for reinforcing escape routes and procedures. Conduct regular drills involving all household members, varying the scenarios to cover different types of emergencies. These drills should include practicing escape routes, using escape ladders or other equipment, and gathering at the designated meeting point. Encourage participation and feedback from all participants, using each drill as an opportunity to identify potential improvements in the plan.

Special considerations should be made for individuals with mobility challenges, children, or pets. Ensure that escape plans account for their specific needs, such as providing additional assistance or equipment to aid their evacuation. Assign responsibilities to capable household members for assisting those who may require extra help, and practice these roles during drills to build confidence and competence.

Escape routes should be kept clear of obstacles at all times to ensure they remain accessible in an emergency. Regularly inspect paths for potential obstructions, such as furniture or clutter, and remove any items that could impede evacuation. Make it a habit to keep doors and windows free of locks or fasteners that could delay escape. Encourage household members to report any changes that might affect escape routes, fostering a culture of vigilance and preparedness.

Incorporate emergency supplies into your escape plan, ensuring they are easily accessible during evacuation. These supplies might include flashlights, first aid kits, and portable chargers for communication devices. Store these items near exits or along escape routes to minimize the time needed to gather them during an emergency. Regularly check and update these supplies to ensure they remain functional and relevant to your needs.

Once outside the home, it is important to have a plan for contacting emergency services and communicating with family members who may not be present. Ensure that all household members know how to call for help and provide essential information, such as the address and nature of the emergency. Consider establishing a communication plan with extended family or friends who can assist in coordinating responses and providing support.

Review and update your escape plan regularly to account for changes in your home or household composition. This might include renovations, new additions to the family, or changes in mobility or health. Continually assess the effectiveness of your plan and make adjustments as needed, using drills and feedback to refine procedures and address potential weaknesses.

# Conducting Regular Drills and Simulations

Conducting regular drills and simulations is vital for the effectiveness of any security strategy. These practices enable individuals and families to rehearse emergency procedures, ensuring that everyone knows their roles and responsibilities when a real crisis occurs. The familiarity gained through repetition can significantly reduce panic and confusion, allowing for swift, decisive action that can save lives and protect property. By incorporating a variety of scenarios, tailored training, and continuous improvement, you create a culture of preparedness and resilience within your household.

Initiating a drill starts with defining clear objectives and scenarios that reflect potential threats. Begin by identifying the types of emergencies most likely to affect your home, such as fires, intrusions, or natural disasters. Create realistic scenarios that simulate these threats, taking into account different times of day and various household dynamics, such as members being asleep or away from home. By addressing a wide range of possibilities, you ensure that drills are comprehensive and adaptable to unexpected situations.

Communication is key during drills, as it ensures that all participants understand the scenario and their specific roles. Start each drill with a briefing that outlines the situation, objectives, and expectations. Use clear, concise language to convey instructions, and provide an opportunity for questions to clarify any uncertainties. Designate a leader, such as a parent or trusted adult, to oversee the drill and facilitate communication among participants.

During the drill, focus on executing the emergency procedures as realistically as possible. Encourage participants to treat the drill with the same seriousness they would a real emergency, following established escape routes, using designated communication methods, and adhering to any safety protocols. For example, in a fire drill, participants should practice crawling low under simulated smoke, using alternative exits if necessary, and gathering at the predetermined meeting point outside. This hands-on practice reinforces knowledge and builds muscle memory, making it more likely that individuals will respond appropriately in an actual emergency.

After completing the drill, conduct a debriefing session to evaluate performance and identify areas for improvement. Encourage participants to share their experiences, challenges, and any observations they made during the exercise. Use this feedback to make adjustments to the emergency plan, addressing any weaknesses or gaps that were identified. For instance, if a participant struggled to open a particular window, consider replacing the mechanism or adding tools to assist with the task. By continuously refining the plan, you increase its effectiveness and reliability.

Incorporate different types of simulations beyond physical drills to enhance preparedness. Tabletop exercises can be an effective way to discuss and analyze scenarios in a low-pressure environment. These discussions allow participants to explore various "what-if" situations, considering how they would respond and what resources they might need. By engaging in these thought experiments, individuals develop critical thinking skills and a deeper understanding of emergency procedures.

Technology can be harnessed to augment drills and simulations, providing additional layers of realism and engagement. Virtual reality (VR) simulations, for example, can immerse participants in a controlled environment that mimics real-world emergencies. These experiences can be particularly valuable for training individuals on how to remain calm and focused under stress, improving their decision-making abilities in high-pressure situations.

Involving all household members in drills and simulations, including children and pets, ensures comprehensive preparation. Tailor exercises to accommodate the unique needs and abilities of each participant, providing additional guidance or assistance as necessary. For example, children may benefit from simplified instructions and reassurance, while pets might require familiarization with the sound of alarms or the use of carriers. By practicing as a cohesive unit, you strengthen the sense of teamwork and mutual support that is crucial in an emergency.

Regularly updating and varying drills helps maintain engagement and ensures the plan remains relevant. Schedule exercises at least twice a year, adjusting the frequency based on the complexity of the plan and the specific needs of your household. Introduce new scenarios over time, incorporating lessons learned from previous drills and any changes in the household or environment.

Establishing a schedule for drills and simulations emphasizes their importance and integrates them into the household routine. Mark these events on the calendar and treat them as essential appointments, demonstrating a commitment to safety and preparedness. Encourage enthusiasm and participation by framing drills as opportunities to learn and improve, rather than as chores or obligations.

# CHAPTER 6

# STOCKPILING ESSENTIAL SUPPLIES

## Building a Long-Term Food Storage System

Building a long-term food storage system is a critical component of disaster preparedness, ensuring that you and your family have access to essential nutrition during times of crisis. This system is designed to provide sustenance over an extended period, allowing you to weather disruptions in food supply chains, natural disasters, or other emergencies that might limit access to fresh groceries. A well-organized storage system not only provides peace of mind but also offers practical benefits in managing household resources efficiently.

The initial step in constructing a long-term food storage system involves assessing your family's dietary needs and preferences. Consider factors such as the number of people in your household, any specific dietary restrictions, and the types of foods you typically consume. This assessment will guide your selection of items to stockpile, ensuring that your storage system is both practical and sustainable. Aim for a diverse array of food items that provide balanced nutrition, including carbohydrates, proteins, fats, vitamins, and minerals.

Dry goods form the backbone of any long-term food storage system, owing to their extended shelf life and ease of storage. Staples such as rice, pasta, beans, and lentils are versatile and nutrient-dense, making them ideal candidates for stockpiling. These items can be stored in airtight containers to protect against pests and moisture, maximizing their longevity. Consider investing in food-grade buckets with gamma seal lids, which offer excellent protection and accessibility.

Canned goods are another essential component of a robust food storage system. They provide a convenient and reliable source of proteins, fruits, vegetables, and even ready-to-eat meals. When selecting canned items, prioritize those that are low in sodium and preservative-free to maintain health and nutrition. Rotate canned goods regularly to ensure freshness, using the first-in, first-out (FIFO) method. This approach involves consuming the oldest items first, thereby preventing spoilage and waste.

Freeze-dried and dehydrated foods are valuable additions to long-term storage, offering extended shelf life and minimal storage space requirements. These items are lightweight and retain much of their original nutritional content, making them an excellent option for emergency preparedness. Freeze-dried fruits, vegetables, and meats can be rehydrated quickly with water, providing convenient meal options. Dehydrated foods, such as jerky or dried fruits, offer ready-to-eat snacks that are both nutritious and satisfying.

Preserving foods at home is an effective way to augment your storage system with items tailored to your taste and dietary preferences. Techniques such as canning, pickling, and fermenting allow you to preserve seasonal produce and extend its shelf life. Properly canned goods, when stored in a cool, dark place, can remain viable for several years. Experimenting with different preservation methods not only diversifies your food supply but also fosters self-reliance and resourcefulness.

Water is a crucial component of any long-term storage plan, as it is essential for both hydration and food preparation. Store at least one gallon of water per person per day, aiming for a minimum two-week supply. Use food-grade containers or commercially bottled water to ensure safety and quality. In addition to stored water, consider investing in a high-quality water filtration system or purification tablets, which can provide safe drinking water in the event that your primary supply is depleted.

Organization is key to maintaining an effective food storage system. Designate a specific area in your home for storage, such as a basement, pantry, or dedicated closet. Ensure that the space is cool, dry, and away from direct sunlight, as these conditions can degrade food quality. Shelving units or racks can help maximize space and improve accessibility, allowing you to easily inventory and rotate items.

Regularly inventory your food storage to track stock levels and expiration dates. This practice enables you to identify gaps in your supply and adjust your purchasing habits accordingly. Use a spreadsheet or dedicated app to streamline this process, making it easier to manage large quantities of items and ensuring that nothing is overlooked. Conducting periodic reviews of your inventory also helps you stay informed about what you have on hand, allowing for efficient meal planning and reducing the risk of waste.

Building a long-term food storage system requires an upfront investment of time and resources, but the benefits far outweigh the initial effort. By curating a diverse and balanced supply of foods, you ensure that your household remains well-nourished during emergencies, while also gaining greater control over your food resources. This preparedness not only enhances your resilience in the face of uncertainty but also fosters a sense of security and self-sufficiency. Through careful planning and ongoing maintenance, your food storage system becomes a valuable asset, providing nourishment and peace of mind for you and your loved ones.

## Water Purification and Storage Solutions

Water purification and storage solutions are essential components of emergency preparedness, ensuring that you have access to safe, potable water in times of crisis. Whether faced with natural disasters, infrastructure failures, or contamination events, having a reliable water supply is crucial for survival. Establishing an effective water storage and purification system involves understanding the potential risks, selecting appropriate methods, and maintaining supplies to meet your household's needs.

The first step in preparing for water emergencies is assessing your household's water requirements. On average, each person needs at least one gallon of water per day for drinking and basic hygiene. However, this amount can vary based on factors such as climate, physical activity, and medical needs. Planning for a minimum two-week supply is advisable, providing a buffer against disruptions in municipal water services or delays in relief efforts.

Storage solutions play a critical role in maintaining an accessible water supply. Commercially bottled water is a convenient option, offering a ready-to-use supply that requires minimal preparation. When purchasing bottled water, check expiration dates and rotate stock regularly to ensure freshness. For larger quantities, consider using food-grade water storage containers, available in sizes ranging from a few gallons to several hundred. These containers should be stored in a cool, dark place to prevent algae growth and degradation.

If you choose to store tap water, ensure it is treated and stored properly to maintain safety. Use clean, sanitized containers with tight-sealing lids to prevent contamination. Adding a few drops of unscented liquid household bleach per gallon can help disinfect the water, though this method should be used cautiously to avoid over-treatment. Clearly label containers with the date of storage and replace the water every six months to prevent stagnation.

In addition to stored water, purification methods are essential for ensuring access to safe drinking water during extended emergencies. Filtration systems, such as gravity-fed filters or pump-operated devices, are effective in removing sediments, bacteria, and protozoa from untreated water sources. These systems are portable and versatile, making them ideal for both home use and outdoor activities. When selecting a filter, verify its specifications to ensure it meets your needs, such as the ability to remove viruses or heavy metals if necessary.

Chemical purification is another option, using tablets or drops to disinfect water. These products typically contain chlorine or iodine, which kill harmful microorganisms. While chemical treatments are effective and lightweight, they may impart an unpleasant taste, which can be mitigated by using flavor enhancers or activated carbon filters. Be sure to follow the manufacturer's instructions for dosage and contact time to ensure effectiveness.

Boiling water is a time-tested purification method, capable of killing most pathogens. Bringing water to a rolling boil for at least one minute (or three minutes at higher altitudes) is sufficient to ensure safety. While boiling is effective, it requires a heat source and can be time-consuming, making it less practical for large volumes or prolonged emergencies.

Ultraviolet (UV) purification devices are increasingly popular for their ability to neutralize bacteria and viruses without altering the taste of the water. These portable devices use UV light to disrupt the DNA of microorganisms, rendering them harmless. UV purifiers are compact and easy to use, though they require batteries or solar power to operate, and their effectiveness can be reduced in cloudy or sediment-laden water.

Maintaining a diverse array of water purification methods enhances your resilience, allowing you to adapt to different scenarios and water sources. Additionally, educating all household members on the proper use and maintenance of these systems is crucial. Regularly inspect and service your equipment, replacing filters or components as needed to ensure functionality.

Incorporating rainwater harvesting into your preparedness plan can supplement stored water supplies. Collecting rainwater from rooftops or other surfaces can provide an additional source of water for non-potable uses, such as gardening or sanitation. Ensure that your collection system includes a means of diverting the first flush of rainwater, which may contain contaminants from the roof. Properly filtering and treating harvested rainwater can make it suitable for drinking, though local regulations should be consulted to ensure compliance.

Community resources can also play a role in water preparedness. Establishing relationships with neighbors or participating in local preparedness groups can facilitate information sharing and mutual support during emergencies. Community-level initiatives, such as shared water storage facilities or cooperative purchasing of purification equipment, can enhance individual and collective resilience.

# Maintaining a Balanced Supply of Essentials

Maintaining a balanced supply of essentials is a cornerstone of effective emergency preparedness, ensuring that you and your family have the necessary resources to endure unforeseen disruptions. A well-rounded stockpile provides a safety net, allowing you to navigate crises with confidence and stability. Achieving this balance requires careful planning, regular assessment, and a thorough understanding of your household's unique needs and preferences.

The foundation of a balanced supply begins with a comprehensive inventory of essential items, including food, water, medical supplies, and personal care products. Start by evaluating your household's daily consumption patterns, identifying the items you rely on most frequently. This assessment will help you determine the quantities needed to sustain your family for an extended period, typically two weeks to several months, depending on your level of preparedness.

Food is a critical component of any stockpile, providing the energy and nutrients required to maintain health and well-being. Prioritize non-perishable items with long shelf lives, such as canned goods, dried fruits, nuts, and grains. These staples offer versatility and can be combined to create a variety of meals. Additionally, consider including freeze-dried or dehydrated foods, which are lightweight and retain much of their nutritional value. When selecting food items, take into account any dietary restrictions or preferences within your household to ensure that everyone is adequately nourished.

Water is another essential element, vital for hydration and food preparation. Store at least one gallon per person per day, with a minimum two-week supply. This amount may need to be adjusted based on local climate conditions and individual needs. In addition to stored water, invest in water purification methods, such as filters or chemical treatments, to ensure access to safe drinking water in the event of contamination or depletion.

Medical supplies are a crucial aspect of a balanced stockpile, enabling you to address minor injuries and illnesses without relying on external resources. Assemble a comprehensive first aid kit, including bandages, antiseptics, pain relievers, and any prescribed medications. Regularly check expiration dates and replenish supplies as needed. Consider adding items such as a thermometer, blood pressure monitor, or glucose meter if relevant to your household's health needs.

Personal care products, such as soap, toothpaste, and hygiene items, should also be included in your stockpile to maintain cleanliness and comfort during an emergency. These items may seem secondary to food and water but play an important role in preserving morale and preventing illness. Assess your family's typical usage and ensure that you have an adequate supply to last through an extended period.

Organization is key to maintaining a balanced supply of essentials. Designate a specific area in your home for storage, ensuring that it is easily accessible and protected from environmental factors such as moisture or pests. Use shelving, bins, or containers to keep items organized and visible, making it easier to monitor stock levels and rotate items as needed. Label containers clearly, indicating contents and expiration dates, to streamline inventory management.

Regularly reviewing and updating your stockpile is essential to ensure its effectiveness and relevance. Conduct periodic inventory checks to assess current supplies and identify any gaps or surplus items. This process allows you to adjust your purchasing habits, focusing on replenishing depleted items and avoiding unnecessary duplicates. Use a checklist or spreadsheet to track your inventory, making it easier to manage large quantities and maintain an accurate overview of your resources.

Incorporating a rotation system is a practical way to keep your stockpile fresh and minimize waste. The first-in, first-out (FIFO) method is commonly used, involving the consumption of older items before newer ones. This approach ensures that perishable goods are used before their expiration dates and helps maintain the quality and safety of your supplies. Encourage household members to participate in the rotation process, fostering a sense of shared responsibility and awareness.

Maintaining a balanced supply also involves staying informed about potential threats and adjusting your stockpile accordingly. Monitor local news and weather reports to anticipate disruptions, such as severe storms or supply chain issues, that may impact your access to essential goods. By proactively addressing these challenges, you can bolster your stockpile and enhance your resilience in the face of uncertainty.

Collaboration with neighbors and community preparedness groups can further support your efforts to maintain a balanced supply of essentials. Sharing information and resources can help mitigate the impact of shortages and foster a sense of solidarity during emergencies. Consider participating in community initiatives, such as bulk purchasing or cooperative storage, to reduce costs and increase access to essential items.

## Rotating Supplies and Managing Expiry Dates

Rotating supplies and managing expiry dates are crucial practices for maintaining the integrity and effectiveness of your stockpile. These actions ensure that your emergency supplies remain fresh, safe, and ready for use when needed. By implementing systematic rotation and diligent monitoring of expiry dates, you maximize the utility of your stockpile and minimize waste, creating a reliable foundation for emergency preparedness.

The concept of rotation is simple yet essential: consume older items before newer ones to prevent spoilage and maintain freshness. This practice is commonly referred to as the first-in, first-out (FIFO) method. By adhering to FIFO, you reduce the risk of items expiring before they are used, which is particularly important for perishable goods such as food, medications, and personal care products.

To implement an effective rotation system, start by organizing your stockpile in a manner that facilitates easy access to the oldest items. Shelving units or storage racks can be arranged so that newer supplies are placed behind older ones, naturally encouraging the use of items in the correct order. Clearly label each item with its purchase or restock date, using a permanent marker or label maker to ensure visibility. This step is especially important for goods with long shelf lives, where expiry dates may not be immediately apparent.

Regular inventory checks are essential for managing expiry dates and ensuring that your stockpile remains viable. Conduct inventory assessments at least once every three to six months, or more frequently if your stockpile includes items with shorter shelf lives. During these checks, examine each item for signs of spoilage or damage, such as bulging cans, leaks, or unusual odors. Remove any compromised items immediately to prevent contamination of other supplies.

In addition to physical inspections, maintain a digital or printed inventory log that tracks the quantity, purchase date, and expiry date of each item. This log serves as a reference for planning meals, restocking supplies, and identifying items that need to be used soon. Spreadsheets or dedicated inventory management apps can simplify this process, providing an at-a-glance overview of your stockpile's status.

Engage all household members in the rotation and inventory process to foster a shared sense of responsibility and awareness. Assign specific tasks, such as labeling, organizing, or recording data, to individuals based on their abilities and interests. This collaborative approach not only streamlines the management of your stockpile but also empowers each person with valuable skills and knowledge.

Understanding the shelf life of different items is key to managing expiry dates effectively. Foods with extended shelf lives, such as canned goods, rice, and pasta, can remain viable for several years if stored properly in a cool, dry environment. However, even these items can degrade over time, losing flavor, texture, and nutritional value. Monitor these goods closely and plan meals around items that are approaching their expiry dates.

For medications and personal care products, expiry dates are particularly important as they can impact the efficacy and safety of these items. Some medications may become less effective or even harmful after their expiry date, making it crucial to adhere to recommended usage guidelines. Regularly review your medication supply, removing expired items and restocking as necessary to ensure you have access to effective treatments during emergencies.

Incorporating meal planning into your routine is an effective way to rotate food supplies and prevent waste. Design weekly or monthly meal plans that utilize items nearing their expiry dates, ensuring that they are consumed before they spoil. This practice not only keeps your stockpile fresh but also reduces grocery bills by minimizing the need for additional purchases. Experimenting with new recipes can add variety and interest to your meals, making it easier to incorporate stockpiled items into your diet.

Donations can be a practical solution for managing surplus items that you are unable to use before their expiry dates. Local food banks, shelters, or community organizations often welcome donations of non-perishable goods, providing you with an opportunity to support those in need while maintaining the integrity of your stockpile. Before donating, ensure that items are unopened, undamaged, and within their expiry dates to maximize their usefulness and safety.

## Preparing for Special Dietary Needs

Preparing for special dietary needs is an essential aspect of stockpiling supplies, ensuring that all members of your household can maintain their health and well-being during emergencies. Whether dealing with allergies, intolerances, medical conditions, or specific dietary preferences, accommodating these needs in your emergency stockpile requires careful planning and attention to detail. By addressing these requirements, you not only safeguard the health of your loved ones but also provide a sense of normalcy and comfort in challenging times.

The first step in preparing for special dietary needs is identifying the specific requirements of each household member. This includes understanding any allergies or intolerances, such as gluten or lactose, as well as dietary preferences, such as vegetarianism or veganism. Additionally, consider any medical conditions that necessitate specific nutritional considerations, such as diabetes or hypertension. Compiling a detailed list of these needs will guide your selection of appropriate supplies and help you create a stockpile that caters to everyone's well-being.

When selecting food items for your stockpile, prioritize those that align with the dietary needs identified. For instance, if someone in your household requires a gluten-free diet, opt for gluten-free grains, pasta, and baking mixes. Similarly, for lactose intolerance, consider stocking lactose-free milk alternatives and dairy-free products. Be diligent in reading labels and researching products to ensure their suitability, as some items may contain hidden allergens or ingredients that conflict with specific dietary requirements.

Diversity is key to maintaining a balanced and appealing stockpile, particularly when accommodating special dietary needs. Aim to include a variety of foods from different food groups, ensuring that nutritional requirements are met. For example, if your household includes vegetarians, incorporate plant-based protein sources such as beans, lentils, tofu, and nuts. Consider freeze-dried or dehydrated fruits and vegetables to provide essential vitamins and minerals while minimizing storage space.

In addition to selecting suitable foods, consider how these items can be combined to create meals that are both nutritious and satisfying. Planning balanced meals that incorporate a range of nutrients can help prevent deficiencies and promote overall health. Experiment with recipes that use stockpiled ingredients, ensuring that they meet the dietary needs of your household while offering variety and enjoyment.

Non-food items can also play a role in accommodating special dietary needs. For instance, if someone requires specific cooking utensils or appliances to prepare their meals, such as a gluten-free toaster or a high-powered blender for pureed foods, ensure that these items are readily available. This consideration extends to personal care products, as some individuals may require hypoallergenic or fragrance-free options to avoid adverse reactions.

Communication is vital when preparing for special dietary needs, both within your household and with external support networks. Ensure that all household members are aware of each other's requirements and preferences, fostering an environment of mutual support and understanding. This awareness can help prevent accidental exposure to allergens or other harmful substances. Additionally, consider informing neighbors or local preparedness groups about any critical dietary needs, as they may be able to offer assistance or share resources during emergencies.

Education and awareness are crucial components of accommodating special dietary needs in your stockpile. Stay informed about the latest research and recommendations related to specific dietary requirements, and consult healthcare professionals or nutritionists as needed. This knowledge can guide your purchasing decisions and help you adapt your stockpile to changing needs or recommendations. Encourage household members to educate themselves about their own dietary requirements, empowering them to make informed choices and contribute to the management of the stockpile.

Flexibility is essential when preparing for special dietary needs, as circumstances and requirements can change over time. Regularly review and update your stockpile to ensure it remains relevant and effective. This process may involve adjusting quantities, introducing new products, or phasing out items that are no longer suitable. Conduct periodic inventory checks to assess the status of your supplies, making note of any items that need replenishment or replacement.

Incorporating supplements into your stockpile can help bridge nutritional gaps, particularly for individuals with restricted diets. Vitamins and minerals, such as vitamin D, calcium, or iron, may be necessary to support overall health. Consult with healthcare professionals to determine the appropriate supplements for each household member, and ensure that these items are stored properly to maintain their efficacy.

Building relationships with local stores, farmers, or specialty food suppliers can enhance your ability to source suitable products for your stockpile. Establishing connections with these vendors may provide access to a wider range of options, including hard-to-find items or bulk purchasing opportunities. Additionally, participating in online forums or social media groups dedicated to specific dietary needs can offer valuable insights, recommendations, and support from others facing similar challenges.

# CHAPTER 7

# IMPLEMENTING OFF-GRID ENERGY SOLUTIONS

## Exploring Solar Power Options

Harnessing the power of the sun is an effective and sustainable approach to achieving energy independence. Solar power options offer a reliable means of providing electricity during emergencies, reducing reliance on traditional power grids, and minimizing environmental impact. By exploring solar energy solutions, you can enhance your home's resilience and ensure a steady supply of electricity, even when external sources fail.

The journey to implementing solar power begins with understanding the various options available. Photovoltaic (PV) systems are the most common type of solar power solution for residential use. These systems convert sunlight directly into electricity using solar panels, which consist of numerous solar cells. The electricity generated can be used immediately, stored in batteries for later use, or fed back into the grid if you have a grid-tied system. Grid-tied systems allow you to benefit from net metering, where excess electricity is sold back to the utility company, potentially reducing your energy bills.

When considering a solar power system, assess your specific energy needs and goals. Calculate your household's average energy consumption by reviewing utility bills and identifying peak usage periods. This information will help determine the size and capacity of the solar power system required to meet your needs. Additionally, consider your location and available sunlight, as these factors influence the efficiency and output of the solar panels. Homes in regions with abundant sunlight can generate more electricity, while those in cloudier areas may require larger systems or supplemental energy sources.

Selecting the right solar panels is a crucial step in implementing an effective solar power solution. Panels vary in efficiency, durability, and cost, so it's important to weigh these factors against your budget and energy goals. Monocrystalline panels are known for their high efficiency and sleek appearance, making them a popular choice for residential use. Polycrystalline panels are typically more affordable but slightly less efficient. Thin-film solar panels offer flexibility and lower costs, but they generally have lower efficiency rates. Consider these options carefully to find the best fit for your home.

In addition to solar panels, a complete solar power system includes other essential components, such as inverters, batteries, and charge controllers. Inverters convert the direct current (DC) electricity produced by the panels into alternating current (AC) electricity, which powers household appliances. Batteries store excess electricity for use during periods of low sunlight or power outages, ensuring a continuous energy supply. Charge controllers regulate the flow of electricity between the panels and batteries, preventing overcharging and prolonging battery life.

Installation is a critical phase in implementing solar power solutions. Hiring a reputable and experienced solar installer is advisable to ensure that the system is set up correctly and safely. The installer will assess your property, design a system tailored to your needs, and handle the necessary permits and approvals. During the installation process, consider the orientation and tilt of the solar panels, as these factors significantly impact their efficiency. Panels should ideally face south in the northern hemisphere or north in the southern hemisphere, with an angle that maximizes exposure to sunlight throughout the year.

Maintaining your solar power system is essential for optimal performance and longevity. Regularly inspect the panels for dirt, debris, or damage, as these can reduce efficiency. Clean the panels as needed, using water and a soft brush or cloth to remove any buildup. Check the system's electrical components, such as inverters and batteries, for signs of wear or malfunction, and address any issues promptly to prevent further damage. Keeping detailed records of maintenance activities can help track system performance and identify trends or potential problems.

Financial incentives and rebates can make solar power systems more affordable and accessible. Many governments and utility companies offer programs that encourage the adoption of renewable energy by providing tax credits, grants, or low-interest loans. Research the incentives available in your area and factor them into your budget and planning. These programs can significantly reduce the upfront costs of solar power systems, making them a more attractive option for homeowners seeking energy independence.

Exploring solar power options not only enhances your home's resilience and security but also contributes to a more sustainable future. By reducing reliance on fossil fuels and decreasing greenhouse gas emissions, solar power systems play a vital role in combating climate change and protecting the environment. Additionally, investing in renewable energy can increase your property's value, as more homebuyers seek energy-efficient and eco-friendly homes.

Integrating solar power with other off-grid energy solutions can further strengthen your home's energy independence. Consider combining solar power with wind turbines, backup generators, or energy storage systems to create a comprehensive and versatile energy network. This approach allows you to diversify your energy sources, reducing the impact of fluctuations in weather conditions or equipment performance.

# Wind Energy and Backup Generators

Harnessing wind energy and utilizing backup generators are vital components of establishing a robust off-grid energy system. These solutions provide reliable power sources independent of conventional electricity grids, ensuring that your home remains functional during emergencies or power outages. By integrating wind energy and backup generators, you can enhance your home's resilience and maintain essential services, regardless of external conditions.

Wind energy, a renewable and sustainable resource, can be an effective addition to your energy strategy. Small-scale wind turbines are designed for residential use, capturing wind power to generate electricity. When considering wind energy, evaluate your location's wind resources, as consistent and strong winds are essential for optimal turbine performance. Coastal areas, open plains, and hilltops typically offer favorable wind conditions, while urban or heavily wooded areas may present challenges due to obstructions.

Selecting the right wind turbine involves assessing factors such as size, capacity, and design. Turbines are available in various sizes, measured in kilowatts (kW), and should be matched to your household's energy needs. Small turbines, ranging from 1 kW to 10 kW, are suitable for most residential applications. Consider the turbine's cut-in speed, which is the minimum wind speed required to generate power, and ensure that it aligns with your location's average wind speeds.

The placement of wind turbines is crucial for maximizing efficiency. Install turbines on tall towers or poles to capture higher altitude winds, which are generally stronger and more consistent. The tower height should be at least 30 feet above any nearby obstacles, such as trees or buildings, to minimize turbulence and optimize energy capture. Professional installation is recommended to ensure structural stability and compliance with local regulations.

Incorporating wind energy into your home's power system requires additional components, such as inverters, batteries, and charge controllers. Inverters convert the direct current (DC) electricity generated by the turbine into alternating current (AC) electricity, suitable for household use. Batteries store excess electricity for periods of low wind or increased demand, providing a continuous energy supply. Charge controllers regulate the flow of electricity between the turbine and batteries, preventing overcharging and extending battery life.

Backup generators serve as a reliable complement to wind energy, providing power during periods of low wind or system maintenance. Generators can run on various fuels, including gasoline, diesel, propane, or natural gas, offering flexibility in resource availability. When selecting a backup generator, consider factors such as power output, fuel type, and runtime. Choose a generator with sufficient capacity to meet your household's essential energy needs, typically measured in watts or kilowatts.

The installation of a backup generator involves strategic placement and connection to your home's electrical system. Position the generator in a well-ventilated area, away from windows and doors, to prevent exhaust fumes from entering the home. Ensure that the generator is protected from the elements, either through a weatherproof enclosure or by situating it in a sheltered location. Professional installation is advisable to ensure safe and efficient integration with your home's electrical system.

To maximize the effectiveness of your off-grid energy solution, consider implementing an automatic transfer switch (ATS). An ATS seamlessly transitions your home's power supply from the grid to the generator in the event of an outage, ensuring uninterrupted service. This device eliminates the need for manual intervention, providing peace of mind and convenience during emergencies.

Regular maintenance is essential for both wind turbines and backup generators to ensure their longevity and performance. For wind turbines, inspect the blades, tower, and electrical components for signs of wear or damage. Clean the turbine blades periodically to remove dirt and debris, which can impact efficiency. Backup generators require routine checks of fuel levels, oil, and filters, as well as periodic testing to verify functionality. Adhering to manufacturer-recommended maintenance schedules can prevent unexpected failures and extend the lifespan of your equipment.

Financial incentives and rebates can help offset the cost of wind energy systems and backup generators. Many governments and utility companies offer programs to promote renewable energy adoption, providing tax credits, grants, or low-interest loans. Research available incentives in your area and incorporate them into your planning and budgeting process. These programs can make off-grid energy solutions more accessible and financially viable for homeowners.

Integrating wind energy and backup generators with other off-grid energy solutions, such as solar power, can further enhance your home's energy independence. This diversified approach allows you to capitalize on multiple renewable resources, mitigating the impact of fluctuations in weather conditions or equipment performance. By creating a comprehensive energy network, you ensure a reliable and resilient power supply for your home.

# Energy Conservation Techniques

Effective energy conservation techniques are pivotal in ensuring the sustainability and efficiency of off-grid energy solutions. By reducing overall energy consumption, you not only prolong the life of your energy resources but also maximize the functionality of your off-grid systems. These techniques can be seamlessly integrated into daily routines, promoting a lifestyle that prioritizes both environmental responsibility and energy independence.

Begin by conducting an energy audit of your home to identify areas where energy is being wasted. This involves analyzing the energy usage of various appliances and systems, as well as evaluating the efficiency of your home's insulation and structural integrity. Simple actions such as sealing drafts around windows and doors, or adding insulation to attics and walls, can significantly reduce the amount of energy needed for heating and cooling. By minimizing heat loss or gain, you lessen the burden on your energy systems, allowing them to operate more efficiently.

Lighting is another area where substantial energy savings can be achieved. Transitioning from traditional incandescent bulbs to energy-efficient LED lighting can reduce electricity consumption by up to 75%. LEDs also have a longer lifespan, which means less frequent replacements and reduced waste. Consider installing dimmer switches or motion sensors to further conserve energy, ensuring that lights are only used when necessary. Taking advantage of natural light by opening curtains or using skylights can also reduce the need for artificial lighting during daylight hours.

Appliance efficiency plays a crucial role in energy conservation. Opt for Energy Star-rated appliances, which are designed to use less energy without sacrificing performance. These appliances often feature advanced technologies such as variable-speed compressors or adaptive defrost controls that optimize energy use. Regular maintenance of appliances, such as cleaning refrigerator coils or replacing air filters, ensures they operate at peak efficiency. Unplugging devices when not in use or using smart power strips can prevent phantom energy loss, which occurs when electronics consume power even in standby mode.

Heating and cooling systems are significant energy consumers, making their optimization essential for conservation. Programmable thermostats allow you to set specific temperature schedules, reducing energy use when heating or cooling is not needed, such as during the night or when the home is unoccupied. Ceiling fans can enhance air circulation, allowing you to raise the thermostat setting in summer or lower it in winter without sacrificing comfort. Regular maintenance of HVAC systems, including cleaning ducts and checking for leaks, ensures they run efficiently and effectively.

Water heating can account for a considerable portion of energy use in a home. Lowering the thermostat on your water heater to 120 degrees Fahrenheit can yield energy savings without compromising on comfort. Insulating water heaters and pipes minimizes heat loss, reducing the energy required to maintain the desired water temperature. Consider installing low-flow fixtures, such as showerheads and faucets, to conserve both water and the energy used to heat it. Solar water heaters are an excellent addition to off-grid systems, utilizing renewable energy to meet water heating needs.

Behavioral changes are an often-overlooked aspect of energy conservation. Simple actions, such as turning off lights when leaving a room, taking shorter showers, or using cold water for laundry, can collectively result in significant energy savings. Encourage all household members to be mindful of their energy use and to adopt habits that prioritize conservation. Educating your family about the impact of their energy choices fosters a culture of responsibility and sustainability.

Energy conservation also involves strategic planning and adaptation. Monitor your energy consumption regularly to identify trends or areas for improvement. This data can guide future decisions regarding energy use and conservation strategies. Stay informed about new technologies or practices that enhance energy efficiency, and be willing to adapt your approach as needed.

Integrating renewable energy sources, such as solar panels or wind turbines, with energy conservation techniques creates a comprehensive approach to achieving energy independence. This combination reduces reliance on traditional power sources and minimizes environmental impact. By balancing energy production with conservation, you create a resilient and sustainable energy system capable of meeting your household's needs.

Financial incentives and rebates for energy efficiency upgrades can make conservation measures more accessible. Many utilities and government programs offer incentives for the installation of energy-efficient appliances, insulation, or renewable energy systems. Research available programs in your area and incorporate them into your planning and budgeting process. These incentives can offset initial costs and expedite the transition to a more energy-efficient home.

# Maintaining Power Independence

Maintaining power independence is a critical aspect of off-grid living, ensuring that your household remains self-sufficient and resilient in the face of disruptions. The journey towards achieving true power independence involves careful planning, resource management, and the integration of multiple energy sources. By understanding and implementing strategies to sustain this autonomy, you can create a reliable energy system that meets your needs without relying on external grids.

The foundation of maintaining power independence lies in a diversified energy approach. Relying on a single source of power can leave you vulnerable to changes in weather, mechanical failures, or resource scarcity. Therefore, integrating a mix of renewable energy sources, such as solar and wind, with traditional backup systems like generators is essential. This combination allows you to harness the strengths of each source, ensuring a steady supply of energy regardless of conditions.

Solar power is a cornerstone of any off-grid energy system. Photovoltaic panels convert sunlight into electricity, providing a renewable and sustainable power source. To maximize their effectiveness, consider the orientation and angle of your solar panels, ensuring they receive maximum sunlight exposure throughout the day. Regular maintenance, including cleaning and inspection, is crucial to maintain their efficiency and prolong their lifespan.

Wind energy complements solar power by providing electricity during periods of low sunlight or at night. Small wind turbines can be installed on your property to capture wind energy and convert it into usable power. The placement of these turbines is critical; they should be positioned at a height and location that maximizes wind exposure while minimizing turbulence from nearby obstacles. As with solar panels, regular maintenance and monitoring are necessary to ensure optimal performance.

Backup generators serve as a reliable fallback option when renewable sources are insufficient. These generators can run on various fuels, such as gasoline, diesel, propane, or natural gas. Selecting the right type of generator depends on factors like fuel availability, storage constraints, and your overall energy strategy. Generators should be used judiciously to conserve fuel and reduce operational costs, making them an ideal supplement rather than a primary power source.

Energy storage plays a pivotal role in maintaining power independence. Batteries store excess electricity generated by your renewable sources, allowing you to draw on this reserve during periods of low production or high demand. Lithium-ion batteries are popular for their efficiency and longevity, but other options, such as lead-acid or flow batteries, may suit different needs and budgets. Regularly monitoring and managing your battery storage ensures that you can maintain a stable power supply at all times.

Efficiency and conservation are key to sustaining power independence. By reducing your energy consumption, you lessen the burden on your system, prolonging its lifespan and reducing costs. Conduct an energy audit to identify areas where you can cut back on usage, such as upgrading to energy-efficient appliances, improving insulation, or adopting energy-saving habits. These efforts not only conserve power but also contribute to a more sustainable and environmentally-friendly lifestyle.

Monitoring and managing your energy system is crucial for maintaining independence. Implementing a comprehensive monitoring solution allows you to track energy production, consumption, and storage in real-time. This data helps you identify trends, optimize performance, and make informed decisions about your energy strategy. By understanding the dynamics of your system, you can adapt to changing conditions and ensure continuous power availability.

Planning for contingencies is an essential part of maintaining power independence. Unexpected events, such as equipment failures or extreme weather, can disrupt your energy supply. Preparing for these scenarios involves having spare parts and tools on hand, as well as a clear plan for troubleshooting and repairs. Establishing relationships with local suppliers and service providers can also provide valuable support when addressing issues that require professional assistance.

Financial planning is another critical aspect of sustaining power independence. While the initial investment in off-grid energy systems can be substantial, the long-term benefits often outweigh the costs. Developing a budget that accounts for installation, maintenance, and potential upgrades ensures that you can continue to support your energy infrastructure over time. Exploring financial incentives, such as tax credits or rebates for renewable energy investments, can help offset initial expenses and make power independence more attainable.

## Troubleshooting Common Issues

Encountering issues with an off-grid energy system is not uncommon, but being equipped with the right troubleshooting skills can make all the difference in maintaining a reliable power supply. Understanding how to identify and resolve common problems ensures that your home remains resilient and self-sufficient.

One of the most frequent issues faced with off-grid systems is inconsistent energy production. This can often be traced back to solar panels or wind turbines not performing at their optimal levels. Start by examining your solar panels for physical obstructions such as dirt, leaves, or snow. These elements can significantly reduce efficiency by blocking sunlight. Cleaning the panels with water and a soft brush can restore their performance. Similarly, wind turbines should be inspected for debris or ice accumulation on the blades, which can impede their rotation. Regular maintenance routines, including inspections and cleanings, can prevent these issues from escalating.

Battery storage issues can also compromise the functionality of your off-grid system. If you notice that your batteries are not holding a charge or depleting rapidly, start by checking the connections. Loose or corroded connections can disrupt the flow of electricity, leading to inefficient charging. Clean any corrosion with a mixture of baking soda and water, and ensure all connections are secure. Additionally, examine the battery's electrolyte levels if you are using lead-acid batteries. Low levels can prevent proper charging and should be topped up with distilled water as needed. Monitoring the health of your batteries with a battery management system can provide insights into their performance and alert you to potential issues before they become critical.

Inverters, which convert DC electricity from solar panels or wind turbines into AC electricity for home use, are another common point of failure. If your inverter is not functioning, check for error codes or warning lights that can indicate the problem. Often, issues stem from overloads or overheating. Ensure that the inverter is not being subjected to loads beyond its capacity and that it is installed in a well-ventilated area to prevent overheating. Resetting the inverter according to the manufacturer's instructions can sometimes resolve minor glitches. If the problem persists, consulting the inverter's manual or contacting technical support may be necessary.

Generators, often used as backup power sources, can also present challenges. If your generator fails to start, check the fuel supply first. Low or contaminated fuel can prevent the generator from operating. Draining old fuel and replacing it with fresh fuel can often rectify this issue. Additionally, inspect the spark plugs and air filters. Dirty or worn spark plugs can impede ignition, while clogged air filters can restrict airflow, both of which can prevent the generator from starting. Regular servicing, including oil changes and component replacements, is essential for keeping generators in good working order.

Voltage fluctuations or power surges can affect the stability of your off-grid system. These issues can arise from sudden changes in energy production or consumption. Installing surge protectors and voltage regulators can help mitigate these fluctuations, protecting your appliances and ensuring a stable power supply. Monitoring your system's voltage output can help you identify patterns or triggers for these fluctuations, allowing you to address them proactively.

Communication issues between components, such as charge controllers, inverters, and monitoring systems, can lead to inefficiencies or failures in your energy system. Ensure that all components are properly connected and compatible with each other. Firmware updates can resolve compatibility issues and improve system performance. If communication problems persist, consulting with the equipment manufacturer or a professional installer can provide solutions tailored to your system's configuration.

Environmental factors, such as extreme weather conditions, can also impact the performance of your off-grid system. High winds, heavy snowfall, or lightning strikes can damage components or disrupt energy production. Installing weather-resistant enclosures and grounding systems can protect your equipment from these elements. Regularly inspecting your system for weather-related damage and taking preventive measures, such as trimming nearby trees or securing loose components, can enhance its resilience.

Understanding the limitations of your off-grid system is crucial for effective troubleshooting. Overloading the system with too many appliances or devices can lead to failures or inefficiencies. Calculate your household's energy needs and ensure that your system is sized appropriately to meet these demands. Implementing energy conservation techniques, such as using energy-efficient appliances or reducing consumption during peak times, can alleviate stress on your system and improve its overall performance.

Documentation and record-keeping are invaluable tools in troubleshooting off-grid energy systems. Maintaining detailed logs of maintenance activities, system performance, and any issues encountered can help identify patterns or recurring problems. This information can guide troubleshooting efforts and inform future decisions about system upgrades or modifications.

# CHAPTER 8

# MASTERING CRISIS COMMUNICATION

## Setting Up Reliable Communication Channels

Establishing reliable communication channels is an essential component of crisis management, ensuring that information flows seamlessly and efficiently during emergencies. In an era where connectivity can be compromised by natural disasters, technological malfunction, or infrastructural failure, having a robust communication plan is vital for maintaining safety, coordination, and situational awareness.

The first step in setting up reliable communication channels is to assess the specific needs of your household or organization. Consider factors such as the size of your group, the geographical area covered, and the types of crises likely to be encountered. This assessment will guide the selection of appropriate communication tools and methods, ensuring that they suit the unique requirements of your situation.

Traditional landline telephones, though often overlooked in the digital age, can serve as a dependable communication channel during crises. Unlike mobile networks, which may become congested or fail entirely during emergencies, landline systems often prove more resilient. Ensure that your landline phone is corded, as cordless phones require electricity and may not function during power outages. Including a landline in your communication strategy adds a layer of redundancy, enhancing overall reliability.

Mobile phones are indispensable for crisis communication, offering portability and convenience. However, their effectiveness depends on network availability and battery life. To mitigate potential issues, maintain a stock of portable chargers or power banks to keep devices operational during extended outages. Additionally, familiarize yourself with offline communication apps that can function without an active internet connection, enabling peer-to-peer messaging through Bluetooth or Wi-Fi Direct. These tools can be invaluable when traditional networks are compromised.

Two-way radios, such as walkie-talkies, provide a practical solution for short-range communication, particularly in areas with limited cellular coverage. These devices allow instant communication between users, making them ideal for coordinating efforts during crises. Consider investing in radios with a sufficient range to cover your operational area, and ensure that all users are trained in their operation. Regular practice sessions can improve proficiency and ensure that communication is swift and effective when needed most.

Satellite phones offer a robust alternative for long-range communication, especially in remote locations or during widespread network failures. By connecting directly to satellites, these devices bypass terrestrial infrastructure, providing reliable communication regardless of local conditions. While satellite phones can be expensive, their reliability makes them a worthwhile investment for those in regions prone to natural disasters or other crises. Evaluate the cost and coverage options offered by various providers to select a plan that aligns with your needs and budget.

Incorporating a system of visual signals or codes can enhance communication when verbal channels are impractical. Pre-established signals, such as colored flags, lights, or hand gestures, can convey critical information quickly and discreetly. These methods are especially useful in noisy environments or when maintaining silence is necessary for safety. Develop and practice a set of signals with your group to ensure that everyone understands and can respond appropriately.

Establish a clear communication hierarchy to streamline information flow and decision-making during crises. Designate primary and secondary points of contact for each communication channel, ensuring that responsibilities are clearly defined and understood. This hierarchy prevents confusion and ensures that critical information reaches the appropriate individuals without delay. Regularly review and update the hierarchy to account for personnel changes or evolving needs.

Create a comprehensive contact list that includes essential personnel, emergency services, and relevant external organizations. Ensure that this list is accessible both digitally and in hard copy, safeguarding against technological failures. Update the contact list regularly to reflect changes in personnel or contact details, and distribute it to all members of your group.

Training and drills are integral to mastering crisis communication. Conduct regular exercises that simulate various emergency scenarios, allowing participants to practice using communication tools and protocols. These drills help identify potential weaknesses in your communication strategy and provide opportunities for improvement. Debriefing sessions following each exercise can further enhance learning and refine your approach.

Information security is a crucial consideration when setting up communication channels. During crises, sensitive information may be transmitted, necessitating measures to protect data integrity and confidentiality. Implement encryption protocols for digital communications, and educate users on best practices for safeguarding information. Avoid transmitting sensitive data over unsecured channels, and establish guidelines for verifying the authenticity of messages.

Utilizing social media platforms can be an effective means of disseminating information during crises, reaching large audiences rapidly. Platforms such as Twitter or Facebook allow for real-time updates and engagement, providing a channel for both official announcements and community interaction. However, it is essential to verify the accuracy of information shared on social media and to maintain a professional and consistent presence. Designate a team or individual responsible for managing social media communications, ensuring that messaging aligns with your overall strategy.

## Using Emergency Radios and Satellite Phones

Effective crisis communication hinges on the ability to maintain clear lines of communication, regardless of the circumstances. Emergency radios and satellite phones are indispensable tools in ensuring that critical information flows smoothly during times of crisis. Their reliability, even in the most challenging conditions, makes them invaluable assets for anyone seeking to master crisis communication.

Emergency radios, often referred to as two-way radios or walkie-talkies, offer a straightforward and dependable means of communication. These devices operate on specific radio frequencies, allowing users to transmit and receive messages over short distances. The simplicity of their operation, combined with their robustness, makes them ideal for use in situations where cellular networks may be compromised or unavailable.

Selecting the right emergency radio requires consideration of several factors, including range, durability, and available features. Range is particularly crucial, as it determines the distance over which users can communicate. While standard models may cover a few kilometers, more advanced options offer extended ranges, which can be vital in expansive or rugged terrains. Durability is another important consideration. Radios designed for emergency use should be able to withstand harsh conditions, including water exposure, dust, and impact. Models with an IP rating provide an indication of their resilience and are worth considering for those expecting to face challenging environments.

Additional features, such as weather alerts, rechargeable batteries, and hands-free operation, can enhance the utility of emergency radios. Weather alerts provide timely updates on changing conditions, allowing users to make informed decisions during a crisis. Rechargeable batteries ensure that radios remain operational for extended periods, while hands-free operation allows users to communicate while keeping their hands free for other tasks.

Training and familiarization with emergency radios are essential for effective use. All potential users should be comfortable operating the devices, including turning them on and off, adjusting volume, and switching channels. Regular practice sessions can improve proficiency and confidence, ensuring that communication remains seamless when it matters most. Establishing clear communication protocols, such as designated channels for specific types of messages or groups, can further streamline information flow and prevent confusion.

Satellite phones, on the other hand, offer a reliable solution for long-range communication, especially in remote areas where traditional networks are unreliable or nonexistent. By connecting directly to satellites orbiting the Earth, these devices provide coverage virtually anywhere, bypassing terrestrial infrastructure that may be compromised during a crisis.

Choosing the right satellite phone involves evaluating factors such as coverage, cost, and additional features. Different providers offer varying levels of coverage, with some focusing on specific regions while others provide global service. It is important to select a provider whose coverage aligns with your anticipated needs. The cost of satellite phones can be significant, both in terms of initial purchase price and ongoing service fees. However, for many, the peace of mind provided by reliable communication justifies the expense. Additional features, such as GPS tracking, data services, and emergency SOS functions, can enhance the functionality of satellite phones, providing additional layers of safety and information.

Familiarity with the operation of satellite phones is crucial for effective crisis communication. Users should be well-versed in basic functions, such as making and receiving calls, sending text messages, and accessing any additional features. Regular testing and practice calls can ensure that users are comfortable with the device and can use it effectively during an emergency.

Integrating emergency radios and satellite phones into a comprehensive communication plan involves several strategic considerations. First, determine the specific needs of your household or organization, including the types of crises you are likely to encounter and the geographical area you need to cover. This assessment will guide the selection of communication tools and ensure that they are tailored to your unique requirements.

Next, establish a clear communication hierarchy, designating primary and secondary points of contact for each device. This hierarchy ensures that information is disseminated efficiently and that critical messages reach the appropriate individuals without delay. Regularly review and update this hierarchy to account for personnel changes or evolving needs.

Training and drills are essential to mastering crisis communication with emergency radios and satellite phones. Conduct regular exercises that simulate various emergency scenarios, allowing participants to practice using the devices and following established protocols. These drills help identify potential weaknesses in your communication strategy and provide opportunities for improvement. Debriefing sessions following each exercise can further enhance learning and refine your approach.

Information security is a crucial consideration when using emergency radios and satellite phones. During crises, sensitive information may be transmitted, necessitating measures to protect data integrity and confidentiality. Implement encryption protocols for digital communications, and educate users on best practices for safeguarding information. Avoid transmitting sensitive data over unsecured channels, and establish guidelines for verifying the authenticity of messages.

Maintaining the functionality of emergency radios and satellite phones requires regular maintenance and testing. For radios, this includes checking battery life, ensuring antennas are secure, and verifying that all channels are clear and operational. Satellite phones require similar attention, including battery checks, software updates, and ensuring that all features are functioning correctly. Regular testing and maintenance can prevent unexpected failures and ensure that your communication devices are ready for use at all times.

The integration of emergency radios and satellite phones into your crisis communication strategy provides a robust framework for maintaining connectivity during emergencies. By understanding the capabilities and limitations of these devices and incorporating them into a well-thought-out communication plan, you can enhance your ability to respond effectively to crises. This preparedness not only enhances your safety and resilience but also fosters a sense of confidence and security, both within your group and the broader community.

# Establishing a Neighborhood Network

Creating a neighborhood network is a proactive approach to crisis communication that fosters community resilience and ensures a coordinated response during emergencies. By establishing strong communication channels within your neighborhood, you enhance the ability to share information, resources, and support, strengthening the collective security and preparedness of the community.

The first step in establishing a neighborhood network is to identify and engage with key stakeholders. These individuals may include neighborhood association leaders, local business owners, and representatives from community organizations. Their involvement is crucial for gaining support and mobilizing resources. Host a meeting to discuss the benefits of a neighborhood network, presenting it as a collaborative effort to enhance safety and preparedness. Encourage open dialogue, allowing participants to voice concerns and ideas, fostering a sense of ownership and commitment.

Next, assess the specific needs and vulnerabilities of your neighborhood. Consider factors such as geographic location, population density, and potential hazards. This assessment will inform the development of tailored communication strategies and protocols. Engage with local emergency services to gain insights into common challenges and best practices, ensuring that your network aligns with broader community efforts.

With a clear understanding of your neighborhood's needs, establish a communication framework that facilitates the flow of information during crises. This framework should include multiple channels to ensure redundancy and reliability. For example, utilize group messaging apps, email lists, and social media platforms to reach a broad audience quickly. Encourage participants to share these communication tools with their neighbors, expanding the network's reach and inclusivity.

Assign roles and responsibilities within the network to streamline communication and decision-making. Designate primary contacts for different areas or blocks, ensuring that each section of the neighborhood has a point of contact for disseminating information. These contacts should be responsible for relaying updates from local authorities, coordinating assistance, and managing resources. Regularly review and update these roles to reflect changes in personnel or neighborhood dynamics.

Training and education are essential components of an effective neighborhood network. Organize workshops or seminars that cover topics such as basic first aid, emergency preparedness, and effective communication strategies. These events can empower residents with the skills and knowledge needed to respond effectively during crises. Additionally, conduct regular drills to practice communication protocols and ensure that all participants are familiar with their roles and responsibilities.

Developing a system for sharing resources and support within the network is crucial for enhancing community resilience. Encourage residents to identify and catalog available resources, such as generators, medical supplies, or expertise in specific areas. Create a centralized database or platform where this information can be accessed and updated, facilitating resource allocation during emergencies. Establish guidelines for the equitable distribution of resources, ensuring that all residents have access to necessary support.

Building trust and fostering relationships within the neighborhood network is vital for its success. Organize social events, such as block parties or community clean-ups, to strengthen bonds and encourage collaboration. These interactions create a sense of camaraderie and mutual support, enhancing the effectiveness of the network during times of crisis. Encourage open communication and transparency, addressing any conflicts or concerns promptly to maintain trust and cohesion.

Leverage technology to enhance the capabilities of your neighborhood network. Implement tools such as emergency alert systems or mobile apps that provide real-time updates and facilitate communication. These technologies can streamline information flow and ensure that residents receive timely and accurate information. However, it is essential to ensure that all participants have access to and are comfortable using these tools, providing training and support as needed.

Regularly evaluate the effectiveness of your neighborhood network, identifying areas for improvement and adaptation. Solicit feedback from participants to gain insights into their experiences and perspectives, using this information to refine communication strategies and protocols. Stay informed about new developments in crisis communication and preparedness, incorporating innovative practices into your network to enhance its resilience and effectiveness.

Collaboration with external organizations and neighboring communities can further strengthen your neighborhood network. Establish partnerships with local government agencies, emergency services, and non-profit organizations to gain access to additional resources and support. Engage with neighboring communities to share best practices and coordinate efforts, creating a regional network that enhances overall resilience.

# Staying Informed During Crises

Information is a lifeline during crises, guiding decisions, shaping responses, and providing reassurance amidst uncertainty. Staying informed is not merely about accessing data; it's about cultivating a network of reliable sources, discerning truth from noise, and effectively communicating what matters. In a world where misinformation can spread as rapidly as facts, mastering the art of staying informed requires both strategy and vigilance.

A crisis can strike unexpectedly, disrupting normal communication channels and creating chaos. One of the first steps in preparing for such events is identifying trustworthy sources of information. Official channels, such as government agencies, local authorities, and emergency services, are typically the most reliable. These entities often have the resources and mandate to provide accurate and timely updates. Familiarize yourself with their communication platforms, such as websites, social media accounts, and alert systems, ensuring you have easy access to them when needed.

Local news outlets, both print and digital, serve as valuable sources of information during crises. They often have on-the-ground reporters who can provide detailed and context-rich updates tailored to your community. Subscribe to their feeds or newsletters, and consider downloading their mobile apps for instant notifications. Additionally, engage with local journalists and reporters on social media platforms, as they often share rapid updates and insights that may not make it to traditional broadcasts.

Social media platforms, while a double-edged sword, are indispensable tools for staying informed. They provide real-time updates and enable direct communication with official sources, community leaders, and fellow residents. However, the speed at which information spreads on these platforms can also lead to the dissemination of false or misleading content. To navigate this landscape effectively, prioritize information from verified accounts and official pages. Use critical thinking to evaluate the credibility of posts, considering the source, context, and supporting evidence before accepting them as fact.

Community networks, including neighborhood associations and local forums, can offer valuable insights during crises. These groups often share firsthand accounts, resource availability, and localized information that may not be covered by larger media outlets. Participating in these networks not only keeps you informed but also strengthens community ties, fostering a collaborative approach to crisis management. Attend meetings, both virtual and in-person, and contribute to discussions, ensuring you remain an active and informed member.

Emergency alert systems, such as those provided by local governments or weather services, deliver critical information directly to your devices. Sign up for these alerts, customizing them to suit your needs and preferences. Many systems offer options for receiving notifications via text, email, or mobile app, allowing you to choose the method that best fits your lifestyle. Test these alerts periodically to ensure they function correctly, and update your contact information as necessary.

Information overload is a common challenge during crises, where the sheer volume of updates can be overwhelming. To manage this, curate a list of essential sources and prioritize their updates. Limit your exposure to non-essential information, and schedule regular breaks from the news cycle to maintain mental well-being. Create a routine for checking updates, allowing you to stay informed without becoming consumed by the constant influx of information.

Verification is a critical component of staying informed. In the rush to disseminate information, errors can occur, and misinformation can take root. Always cross-reference important updates with multiple sources, seeking confirmation from trusted authorities. Be particularly skeptical of sensational headlines or posts that lack supporting details. When in doubt, wait for further verification before taking action or sharing the information with others.

Communication plays a vital role in staying informed, especially within family or community settings. Establish a system for sharing updates and information, ensuring that everyone remains on the same page. Designate a point person responsible for monitoring key sources and relaying important updates to the group. This approach not only streamlines communication but also reduces the risk of misinformation spreading within your circle.

In the digital age, technological tools can enhance your ability to stay informed. Consider using news aggregator apps that compile updates from multiple sources, providing a comprehensive overview of the situation. These apps often allow for customization, letting you focus on specific topics or regions of interest. Additionally, set up alerts or notifications for keywords related to the crisis, ensuring you receive relevant updates as they occur.

Engaging with experts and professionals can provide deeper insights during crises, offering context and analysis that go beyond surface-level updates. Follow experts in relevant fields, such as meteorologists, health officials, or security analysts, on social media or through their publications. These individuals can offer valuable perspectives, helping you understand the implications of unfolding events and make informed decisions.

Preparation is key to staying informed, and this includes having contingency plans for potential disruptions in communication channels. Equip your home with alternative communication tools, such as battery-powered radios or satellite phones, to ensure you remain connected even if digital networks fail. Familiarize yourself with their operation and test them regularly, ensuring they are ready for use when needed.

Finally, reflect on past experiences to refine your approach to staying informed. Consider what worked well and what could be improved, and adjust your strategies accordingly. Engage in discussions with others about their experiences, sharing lessons learned and best practices. This continuous learning process enhances your ability to navigate future crises with confidence and resilience.

# Developing Communication Protocols

Developing effective communication protocols is vital for managing crises and ensuring that vital information reaches the right people at the right time. Protocols serve as a blueprint for action, guiding how messages are transmitted, who is responsible for communication, and what channels are used. Establishing clear and efficient protocols not only enhances the timeliness and accuracy of information but also helps to reduce confusion and panic during emergencies.

The foundation of any communication protocol is a well-defined chain of command. This hierarchy delineates who is responsible for making decisions and conveying messages. Identifying key personnel who will serve as points of contact is essential. These individuals should possess strong communication skills, the ability to remain calm under pressure, and a comprehensive understanding of the crisis at hand. Once the chain of command is established, ensure that all members of the organization or household are aware of and understand their roles within this framework.

Communication protocols must be tailored to the specific needs and characteristics of your organization or community. Start by conducting a risk assessment to identify potential crises that may arise and consider their impact on communication. This assessment will inform the development of protocols that are relevant and effective. Consider factors such as the size of your group, the physical environment, and the technological infrastructure available when designing your communication strategy.

A critical aspect of effective communication protocols is the selection of appropriate channels for transmitting information. Multiple channels should be utilized to ensure redundancy and reach different audiences. These channels may include email, text messages, phone calls, social media, and in-person briefings. Each has its strengths and limitations, so it's important to choose the right mix based on the context of the crisis and the preferences of your audience. For instance, text messages and social media may be ideal for rapid updates, while in-person briefings can provide more detailed explanations and foster dialogue.

Crafting clear and concise messages is crucial for effective crisis communication. Information should be accurate, relevant, and free of jargon or technical language that may confuse recipients. Develop templates or guidelines for message content, ensuring consistency and clarity in communication. These templates can include key points, such as the nature of the crisis, actions being taken, and any instructions or safety measures for recipients to follow. Regularly review and update these templates to reflect current best practices and lessons learned from past experiences.

Timing is another critical element of communication protocols. During a crisis, the speed at which information is disseminated can significantly impact outcomes. Establish timelines for how quickly messages should be transmitted following a crisis event. These timelines should be realistic, taking into account the time needed to verify information and draft messages, while also recognizing the urgency of the situation. Timely communication helps to mitigate anxiety and provide reassurance to those affected by the crisis.

Training and drills are essential for ensuring that communication protocols are well understood and can be executed effectively. Conduct regular exercises that simulate various crisis scenarios, allowing participants to practice their roles and responsibilities. These drills help to reinforce the importance of following established protocols and provide opportunities to identify and address any weaknesses in the communication strategy. After each exercise, conduct debriefing sessions to gather feedback and refine protocols as needed.

Feedback loops are an important component of any communication protocol. Establish mechanisms for receiving and incorporating feedback from those involved in or affected by the crisis. This feedback can provide valuable insights into the effectiveness of communication efforts and highlight areas for improvement. Encourage open and honest communication, creating a culture that values continuous learning and adaptation.

Maintaining accurate and up-to-date contact information is vital for ensuring that communication protocols function smoothly. Regularly review and update contact lists, ensuring that all key personnel and stakeholders are included. Consider using digital tools or platforms to manage and distribute contact information, making it easily accessible to those who need it. This ensures that messages can be transmitted quickly and efficiently, reducing the risk of delays or miscommunication.

Incorporating technology into communication protocols can enhance their effectiveness and reach. Consider using communication platforms or software that allow for mass notifications, real-time updates, and data sharing. These tools can streamline communication efforts and ensure that information is disseminated to large audiences quickly. However, it's important to ensure that all users are familiar with and comfortable using these technologies, providing training and support as needed.

Establishing protocols for managing misinformation is increasingly important in today's digital age. Rapidly spreading false information can exacerbate crises and undermine trust in official communication. Develop strategies for monitoring and addressing misinformation, including designating personnel to track social media and other channels for inaccuracies. When misinformation is identified, respond promptly with accurate information, using the same channels to reach affected audiences.

# CHAPTER 9

# PREPARING FOR MEDICAL EMERGENCIES

## Building a Comprehensive First Aid Kit

A comprehensive first aid kit is an essential component of any preparedness plan, providing the tools and supplies needed to address medical emergencies effectively. Whether you're at home, in the workplace, or traveling, having a well-stocked first aid kit can make a significant difference in the outcome of an injury or illness. Building a kit that meets your specific needs involves understanding potential risks, selecting appropriate supplies, and ensuring that everyone who might use the kit is familiar with its contents.

Begin by assessing the risks and needs specific to your environment and lifestyle. Consider factors such as the number of people who may require assistance, the types of activities you engage in, and any known medical conditions or allergies. This assessment will guide you in selecting the items that are most relevant and necessary for your situation. For example, a household with children might prioritize items for treating scrapes and bruises, while an outdoor enthusiast might focus on supplies for managing insect bites and sprains.

Once you've identified your needs, it's time to gather the essential items for your first aid kit. Start with the basics, which include adhesive bandages in various sizes, sterile gauze pads, adhesive tape, and antiseptic wipes or solutions. These items are crucial for cleaning and protecting wounds, preventing infection, and promoting healing. Include a pair of non-latex gloves to protect both the caregiver and the injured person from potential contaminants.

Pain relief and fever reducers, such as ibuprofen or acetaminophen, are important additions to any first aid kit. These medications can alleviate discomfort and reduce inflammation, making them useful for a variety of ailments. Be sure to include any prescribed medications for individuals with known medical conditions, and store them in their original packaging to ensure proper dosing and identification.

In addition to basic wound care supplies and medications, your first aid kit should contain tools for managing more serious injuries. Scissors or trauma shears are essential for cutting clothing or gauze, while a thermometer allows you to monitor body temperature accurately. A pair of tweezers is useful for removing splinters or debris from wounds, and a CPR mask or face shield is vital for performing resuscitation safely.

Consider including items that address specific environmental risks. If you live in an area prone to insect bites or stings, include an antihistamine or an epinephrine auto-injector for those with severe allergies. If you're in a region with a high risk of sun exposure, add sunscreen and aloe vera gel to soothe sunburns. Cold packs can be valuable for reducing swelling from sprains or bruises, while heat packs may help alleviate muscle tension or cramps.

Organization is key to ensuring that your first aid kit is easy to use in an emergency. Use a durable, waterproof container to protect the contents from damage and moisture. Label sections or compartments within the container to categorize items, making it easier to locate what you need quickly. Consider creating an inventory list that details the contents of the kit, along with expiration dates for any medications or perishable items. This list should be updated regularly to ensure that supplies remain current and complete.

Training and familiarity with the use of first aid supplies are crucial for effective response during a medical emergency. Consider taking a first aid and CPR course to gain practical skills and confidence in using the items in your kit. Encourage family members, coworkers, or anyone else who may need to access the kit to participate in training as well. Knowledge of basic first aid principles can be invaluable in a crisis, enabling you to provide assistance until professional medical help arrives.

Regular maintenance of your first aid kit ensures that it remains a reliable resource. Schedule periodic checks to review the contents and replace any expired or depleted items. Pay particular attention to medications, as they may lose potency or become unsafe to use past their expiration dates. Restock supplies that have been used, and adjust the contents of the kit as needed to reflect any changes in your health needs or environment.

Accessibility is another important consideration when building a first aid kit. Ensure that it is stored in a location that is easy to reach and known to all potential users. In a household setting, this might be a central location such as the kitchen or bathroom. In a workplace, consider placing kits in common areas or near exits for quick access. If you travel frequently, keep a portable version of your first aid kit in your vehicle or backpack, ensuring that you're prepared wherever you go.

## Stockpiling Essential Medications

Stockpiling essential medications is a strategic measure that ensures continuity of care during medical emergencies, providing a safety net when access to pharmacies or healthcare facilities is disrupted. This preparation involves careful planning, taking into account personal health needs, storage considerations, and the potential longevity of a crisis. By maintaining a reserve of necessary medications, you safeguard your well-being and that of your loved ones in uncertain times.

The first step in stockpiling medications is identifying which ones are essential for your health and daily functioning. Begin by making a comprehensive list of all prescribed medications, over-the-counter drugs, and supplements you or your family members require. Prioritize medications used to manage chronic conditions such as diabetes, hypertension, asthma, or mental health disorders, as these are often critical to maintaining health and preventing complications. Include any medications that might be needed in an emergency, such as pain relief or allergy medication, ensuring that your stockpile is both comprehensive and tailored to your specific needs.

Consult with healthcare providers to determine appropriate quantities for stockpiling. Discuss your intention to build a reserve and seek advice on how much medication you should aim to have on hand. Physicians may provide prescriptions for larger quantities or authorize early refills, especially if they understand the rationale behind your preparation. Pharmacists can offer guidance on managing refills and ensuring that your stockpile remains within safe and legal limits.

When acquiring medications, consider the expiration dates and storage requirements. Medications lose potency over time, and some may become unsafe to use after their expiration date. Organize your stockpile using the "first-in, first-out" method, where older medications are used before newer ones, ensuring that your supply remains fresh. Pay attention to storage conditions, as some medications may require refrigeration or protection from light and humidity. Follow the manufacturer's guidelines to preserve their efficacy and safety.

For those taking multiple medications, a pill organizer or medication log can be invaluable. These tools help manage daily dosages and track which medications have been used, reducing the risk of missed doses or accidental duplication. Keep records of expiration dates and refill schedules, using reminders or alarms to prompt timely replenishment. This level of organization is particularly beneficial during emergencies when stress and disruptions can lead to oversights.

In addition to prescription medications, consider stockpiling over-the-counter medications that address common ailments and symptoms. Pain relievers, fever reducers, antacids, and cold remedies are useful to have on hand, providing immediate relief for minor health issues. Ensure that your stockpile includes a variety of options, catering to different family members' needs and preferences, such as liquid formulations for children or non-drowsy options for daytime use.

Supplements and vitamins can also play a role in maintaining health during emergencies, especially if access to fresh food is limited. Consult with healthcare providers about which supplements might be beneficial for your circumstances, considering factors such as age, dietary restrictions, and existing health conditions. While supplements are not a substitute for a balanced diet, they can help bridge nutritional gaps when resources are scarce.

For those with specific medical devices or equipment, such as inhalers, insulin pumps, or blood glucose monitors, ensure that your stockpile includes necessary supplies and accessories. This might involve having extra batteries, test strips, or replacement parts available, ensuring that these devices remain functional throughout a crisis. Regularly check and maintain equipment to confirm that it is in working order and ready for use.

Communication with your healthcare providers is crucial for successful medication stockpiling. Keep them informed about your plans and any changes to your medication regimen, and seek their advice on managing your stockpile effectively. They can provide valuable insights and support, ensuring that your efforts are aligned with your overall health plan.

Consider potential barriers to stockpiling, such as insurance limitations or cost constraints. Some insurance plans may restrict the quantity of medication that can be dispensed at once, posing challenges for building a reserve. In such cases, explore options such as mail-order pharmacies, which often allow for larger quantities, or generic alternatives that may be more affordable. Communicate openly with your insurance provider to understand your options and work within their guidelines.

Incorporate medication stockpiling into broader emergency planning efforts. Discuss your plans with family members or caregivers, ensuring they are familiar with the location and use of the stockpile. Involve them in the process of maintaining and updating the stockpile, fostering a shared responsibility for preparedness. Consider integrating medication planning into other aspects of emergency readiness, such as evacuation plans or travel preparations, ensuring that your health needs are consistently prioritized.

# Learning Basic Medical Skills

Understanding basic medical skills can be a lifesaver in emergencies. When immediate professional help isn't available, knowing how to respond with practical medical know-how can make a crucial difference. Learning these skills empowers individuals to handle common injuries and illnesses, providing essential aid until professional medical care can be accessed. Through a combination of education, practice, and preparedness, anyone can develop the competence needed to effectively manage medical emergencies.

The journey toward acquiring basic medical skills begins with a commitment to learning. Enrolling in a certified first aid and CPR course is an excellent starting point. These courses typically cover a range of topics, from performing cardiopulmonary resuscitation and using an automated external defibrillator, to managing choking incidents and treating wounds. By participating in hands-on training, you gain not only theoretical knowledge but also practical experience, which is invaluable in real-world situations. Organizations such as the American Red Cross and local community centers frequently offer these courses, making them accessible to a wide audience.

Beyond formal training, self-education plays a pivotal role in building medical skills. Numerous resources, including books, online tutorials, and instructional videos, provide guidance on various aspects of first aid and emergency care. Focus on learning how to assess different types of injuries and illnesses, understanding when it is safe to administer aid, and recognizing when professional medical intervention is necessary. Common topics include handling fractures, burns, allergic reactions, and heat-related illnesses. By diversifying your sources of knowledge, you gain a well-rounded understanding of how to address a variety of medical scenarios.

Practice is key to retaining and effectively applying medical skills. Regularly review and practice what you have learned, whether through refresher courses or simulated exercises. These activities reinforce your knowledge and boost your confidence in applying it. Consider organizing practice sessions with family members or friends, creating scenarios that mimic potential emergencies. This collaborative approach not only enhances individual skills but also fosters a sense of teamwork and preparedness within your community.

Understanding how to use the contents of a first aid kit is another fundamental aspect of basic medical skills. Familiarize yourself with the items typically found in a kit, such as bandages, antiseptics, and medical tape, and learn how to use them effectively. Practice assembling and disassembling a first aid kit, ensuring that you can quickly locate and utilize supplies when needed. Consider customizing your kit to include additional items that address specific needs or risks unique to your environment, such as insect repellent or allergy medication.

Recognizing the signs and symptoms of common medical emergencies is crucial for timely and effective intervention. Learn to identify conditions such as heart attacks, strokes, and seizures, understanding the appropriate response for each. This knowledge allows you to act swiftly, providing critical support that can stabilize the individual until professional help arrives. Pay attention to changes in consciousness, difficulty breathing, or abnormal behavior, as these can be indicators of serious medical issues that require immediate attention.

Communication is an essential component of managing medical emergencies, particularly when interacting with emergency services or healthcare providers. Practice conveying clear and concise information about the situation, including the nature of the injury or illness, the individual's condition, and any actions already taken. This information is vital for ensuring that the individual receives appropriate and timely care. Additionally, effective communication helps to maintain calm and reassure those involved, reducing anxiety and confusion during a crisis.

In addition to physical skills, cultivating a mindset of preparedness and calm is vital in emergency situations. Stress and panic can hinder decision-making and effectiveness, so it is important to practice remaining composed under pressure. Techniques such as deep breathing or mindfulness exercises can help manage stress and maintain focus. By developing mental resilience, you enhance your ability to respond effectively and make sound decisions, even in high-pressure situations.

Engaging with your community can further enhance your medical preparedness. Participate in local initiatives or groups focused on health and safety, sharing knowledge and experiences with others. This involvement not only broadens your skills but also strengthens community ties, creating a network of support that can be invaluable in an emergency. Attend workshops, seminars, or events that focus on health education, and encourage others to do the same, fostering a culture of readiness and collaboration.

Continuing education is an important aspect of maintaining and expanding your medical skills. Stay informed about new developments or guidelines in first aid and emergency care, ensuring that your knowledge remains current. Consider pursuing advanced training opportunities, such as wilderness first aid or advanced cardiac life support, to deepen your expertise. This ongoing commitment to learning enhances your ability to provide effective care and reinforces the importance of preparedness in your everyday life.

## Managing Health Conditions Without Assistance

Managing health conditions without assistance requires foresight, self-reliance, and a comprehensive understanding of one's medical needs. When living alone or in situations where immediate help isn't available, it becomes crucial to develop strategies that ensure proper care and mitigate risks associated with chronic illnesses or sudden health issues. Through proactive planning and the acquisition of essential skills, individuals can navigate their health challenges independently, maintaining well-being and confidence.

Understanding your health condition thoroughly is the first step in managing it independently. This involves educating yourself about the nature of the condition, its symptoms, potential complications, and the treatment options available. Engage with healthcare professionals to gain insights and ask questions that clarify your understanding. This knowledge empowers you to recognize changes in your condition promptly, enabling timely intervention and preventing escalation.

Developing a personalized health management plan is essential for maintaining control over your condition. This plan should outline daily routines, medication schedules, dietary considerations, and any necessary lifestyle modifications. For instance, individuals with diabetes might include regular blood sugar monitoring, insulin administration, and carbohydrate tracking in their plan. Keep this plan accessible and review it regularly, making adjustments as your health needs evolve or as advised by your healthcare provider.

Medication management is a critical aspect of living independently with a health condition. Organize medications using a pill organizer or a medication management app, setting reminders for dosages and refills. Keeping an updated list of prescriptions, including dosages and the purpose of each medication, can be invaluable during medical appointments or emergencies. Familiarize yourself with potential side effects and interactions, ensuring you can identify adverse reactions and seek medical advice when necessary.

Monitoring your health through regular self-assessments is another key component of independent management. Depending on your condition, this could involve tracking vital signs such as blood pressure, heart rate, or glucose levels. Keeping a health journal where you record these metrics, along with notes on symptoms or lifestyle factors, can help identify patterns or triggers that may require attention. This ongoing documentation provides a comprehensive overview of your health status, facilitating informed discussions with healthcare providers.

Establishing a support network, even if you're managing your condition independently, can provide invaluable assistance. Share your health management plan with trusted family members, friends, or neighbors, ensuring they are aware of your condition and how they might assist in an emergency. Having someone check in on you periodically can offer peace of mind and provide a safety net should complications arise. Additionally, consider joining support groups, either locally or online, where you can connect with others facing similar challenges, share experiences, and exchange advice.

Emergency preparedness is crucial for those managing health conditions on their own. Identify potential risks associated with your condition and develop contingency plans. This might include knowing when to seek emergency medical care, having a readily accessible list of emergency contacts, and knowing the location of the nearest healthcare facility. Keep a well-stocked first aid kit and any necessary medical supplies within easy reach, ensuring you can address minor issues promptly.

Nutrition and physical activity play significant roles in managing many health conditions. Tailor your diet to support your specific health needs, incorporating guidelines provided by nutritionists or healthcare providers. For instance, individuals with hypertension might focus on reducing sodium intake, while those with osteoporosis may prioritize calcium and vitamin D. Regular physical activity, adapted to your abilities and limitations, can enhance overall health and well-being, positively impacting your condition.

Developing stress management techniques is vital for maintaining both physical and mental health. Chronic stress can exacerbate many health conditions, making it important to incorporate strategies such as mindfulness, meditation, or gentle exercise into your routine. Establish a relaxing bedtime routine to ensure adequate sleep, as rest is a crucial component of recovery and health maintenance. By managing stress effectively, you enhance your ability to cope with the demands of independent health management.

Staying informed about advancements in the management of your condition can provide new avenues for care and improvement. Regularly consult reputable sources of medical information, such as healthcare provider updates or medical journals, to stay abreast of new treatments, therapies, or recommendations. Discuss these advancements with your healthcare provider to determine their applicability and integrate beneficial changes into your management plan.

Adapting your living environment to accommodate your health needs is an important consideration for independent management. This might involve modifying your home to improve accessibility or reduce hazards, such as installing grab bars in the bathroom or using pill dispensers with larger print for ease of use. Ensure that your home setup supports your health routines, including having a designated space for medication storage and a comfortable area for exercise or relaxation.

# Keeping Records and Medical Information Accessible

In the realm of healthcare, access to accurate and up-to-date information can mean the difference between life and death. Thus, keeping comprehensive and accessible records is paramount for effective medical management, particularly during emergencies. While it may seem daunting, the process is straightforward and can be life-saving. It ensures that individuals receive prompt, efficient, and appropriate care, which is crucial in emergencies where time is of the essence.

The journey to creating a reliable medical record system begins with organization. Start by gathering all necessary documents, such as medical records, insurance policies, and identification. Place copies of these documents in two secure locations—one at home and one outside, like with a trusted friend or in a safe deposit box. Ensure that these records are protected from damage by storing them in waterproof and fireproof containers, which can be purchased online or at retail stores. You may also want to consider using a fireproof safe for extra security.

Personal medical records should include fundamental details such as full name, date of birth, and emergency contact information. In addition, documentation should include what medications are being taken, any allergies, chronic conditions, recent medical procedures, and health insurance information. If you have a complicated medical history, it may be wise to keep a medical summary to provide a quick overview for medical professionals. This can be a lifesaver if you're unable to communicate effectively.

A medical ID card or bracelet with important information can be a lifesaver during emergencies. These items can help healthcare providers quickly identify allergies, chronic conditions, or other critical health concerns. Medical ID cards should be regularly updated, and you should inform your doctor about any changes. You can easily find these cards online, or you can ask your healthcare provider to assist in filling them out.

A digital backup of medical records is also highly recommended. Many platforms and applications allow users to store medical records securely—even offering cloud storage solutions. These systems can be lifesaving during emergencies or in a situation where critical health data is needed quickly. While digital records offer great accessibility, ensure that they are encrypted and stored securely. In addition, it's essential to ensure that family members know how to access your digital records in case of an emergency.

Creating a comprehensive, easily accessible medical file is an important task that should not be overlooked. A medical information booklet should be available at all times, detailing the person's complete medical history. The records should include a list of medical conditions, allergies, and any procedures undergone. It is also important to include a list of current medications, as well as any allergies to medications. In addition, ensure that the person's medical history is up-to-date and includes any recent procedures.

When organizing files, use a simple and effective system to make retrieval as easy as possible. Consider creating a separate folder for each condition, and organizing documents in chronological order. This will help make it easier to find information when needed. Additionally, it is important to keep records up to date and to review them regularly.

In addition to medical records, it is important to keep copies of important documents, such as insurance policies, medical bills, and other important documents. These should be kept in a safe place and should be updated regularly. It is also important to keep copies of important documents, such as birth certificates, marriage certificates, and other important documents.

# CHAPTER 10

# MAINTAINING SANITATION AND HYGIENE

## Effective Waste Management Solutions

Sanitation and hygiene are critical components of maintaining a secure and resilient home environment, especially when circumstances force you to rely on your own resources for extended periods. Effective waste management solutions are essential not only for health reasons but also to ensure a comfortable and livable space. Proper waste disposal minimizes the risk of disease, reduces odors, and contributes to overall safety and peace of mind.

Begin by understanding the types of waste your household generates. This can include organic waste, such as food scraps and yard trimmings, inorganic materials like plastics and metals, and hazardous waste like batteries and chemicals. Each category requires specific management strategies to ensure that waste is handled safely and efficiently. Segregating waste at the source is a fundamental step, as it simplifies disposal and enhances the effectiveness of your waste management system.

Organic waste can be managed effectively through composting, a sustainable practice that converts food scraps and yard waste into nutrient-rich soil. Composting not only reduces the volume of waste in landfills but also provides a valuable resource for gardening and landscape maintenance. Create a composting system that suits your space, whether it be a simple pile, a bin, or a more advanced tumbler. Ensure that you maintain a balance of green materials (like vegetable peels) and brown materials (such as dried leaves) to foster efficient decomposition. Regularly turning the compost pile will aerate it and speed up the process, resulting in rich compost ready for use.

For inorganic waste, such as metals, plastics, and glass, recycling is the most effective method of disposal. Set up a designated area in your home to collect recyclable materials, and familiarize yourself with local recycling programs and guidelines. Some areas offer curbside recycling services, while others may require you to transport recyclables to a collection facility. Be sure to clean and sort materials according to local regulations to ensure they are processed correctly. Reducing the use of non-recyclable materials by opting for reusable or biodegradable alternatives can also significantly decrease the volume of waste your household generates.

Hazardous waste requires careful handling to prevent environmental contamination and health risks. Batteries, electronics, chemicals, and certain cleaning agents fall into this category. Research local hazardous waste disposal facilities and programs, which often offer special collection days or drop-off points for safe disposal. Never dispose of hazardous waste in regular trash or down the drain, as this can cause harm to both the environment and your household.

In situations where traditional waste disposal services are unavailable, consider alternative solutions such as incineration or burying waste. Incineration can be an effective method for reducing waste volume, but it must be done with caution to avoid releasing harmful emissions. Use a controlled burn in a safe location, ensuring that only appropriate materials are incinerated. When burying waste, select a site away from water sources and dig a deep pit to prevent scavenging by animals. Cover the waste thoroughly with soil to minimize odors and pests.

Sanitation doesn't end with waste disposal; maintaining hygiene in prolonged emergencies requires careful planning and execution. Establish a routine for regular cleaning and disinfection, focusing on high-touch surfaces and areas prone to contamination. Use cleaning agents such as bleach solutions or alcohol-based sanitizers to eliminate bacteria and viruses. Ensure that you have a sufficient supply of cleaning materials and personal protective equipment, like gloves and masks, to safeguard against infection.

Personal hygiene is equally important in maintaining a healthy living environment. Regular handwashing with soap and water is one of the most effective ways to prevent illness. When water is scarce, use hand sanitizers containing at least 60% alcohol. Establish a supply of personal hygiene products, including soap, shampoo, toothpaste, and feminine hygiene products, to last through extended periods of isolation. Rotate stock to ensure that products remain fresh and effective.

Addressing waste management and hygiene also involves considering the environmental impacts of your practices. Strive to minimize waste generation by choosing products with minimal packaging and opting for refillable or bulk options when available. Utilize eco-friendly cleaning products that are safe for both your household and the environment. Consider the use of greywater recycling systems to conserve water, particularly in arid regions or during water shortages. Greywater, which is gently used water from sinks, showers, and laundry, can be repurposed for irrigation and flushing toilets, reducing the demand on fresh water supplies.

# Disease Prevention and Control

Disease prevention and control form the backbone of maintaining a healthy and secure home environment, especially when one must rely on limited resources or face disruptions in public health services. The implementation of effective strategies to prevent the spread of illness within your home is crucial to ensuring the well-being of all residents. By adopting a proactive approach, you can mitigate the risks posed by communicable diseases and maintain a sanctuary of health and resilience.

A fundamental aspect of disease prevention is understanding the modes of transmission. Diseases can spread through direct contact, airborne particles, contaminated surfaces, and vectors such as insects. By recognizing these pathways, you can implement targeted measures to disrupt them and prevent the onset of illness. Begin by establishing a rigorous regimen of personal hygiene practices. Regular handwashing with soap and water is a simple yet powerful defense against the spread of pathogens. For situations where water is scarce, keep a supply of alcohol-based hand sanitizers, ensuring they contain at least 60% alcohol for effectiveness.

Surface disinfection is another critical element. High-touch areas such as doorknobs, light switches, and countertops can harbor germs and facilitate their spread. Clean and disinfect these surfaces regularly using effective cleaning agents such as bleach solutions or commercially available disinfectants. Pay special attention to shared spaces like kitchens and bathrooms, as these are common areas where germs proliferate. In addition to routine cleaning, establish a protocol for deep cleaning during outbreaks or when a household member exhibits symptoms of illness.

Personal protective equipment (PPE) plays a vital role in disease control, particularly when caring for sick individuals or during outbreaks. Stock up on essential PPE items such as gloves, masks, and eye protection, and familiarize yourself with their correct usage. Masks, for instance, should cover both the nose and mouth and fit snugly against the sides of the face without gaps. Equip each household member with a personal supply and ensure that used PPE is disposed of properly to prevent cross-contamination.

Ventilation is an often-overlooked factor in controlling airborne diseases. Improving airflow within your home can help dilute and remove airborne pathogens, reducing the risk of transmission. Open windows and doors when weather permits, and utilize fans to enhance air circulation. In spaces where natural ventilation is limited, consider using air purifiers equipped with HEPA filters to capture airborne particles, including viruses and bacteria.

Isolation and quarantine are critical measures when dealing with contagious diseases. If a family member falls ill, establish a designated isolation area where they can recover without exposing others to the illness. This area should be equipped with the necessary amenities to minimize movement throughout the house. Provide the isolated individual with personal items such as utensils and linens, and ensure that they wear a mask when interaction with others is unavoidable. Quarantine protocols should also be in place for individuals who have been exposed to a contagious disease but are not yet symptomatic, to prevent potential spread.

Vaccination remains one of the most effective tools in disease prevention. Ensure that all household members are up-to-date with recommended vaccines, including seasonal flu shots and other relevant immunizations. This not only protects individuals but also contributes to community immunity, reducing the overall spread of disease. Keep a record of vaccinations and consult healthcare providers to address any questions or concerns regarding vaccine safety and efficacy.

Diet and nutrition can significantly influence the body's ability to resist infection. A balanced diet rich in vitamins and minerals strengthens the immune system, enhancing its ability to fight off pathogens. Prioritize the consumption of fresh fruits, vegetables, lean proteins, and whole grains, and consider supplements to fill nutritional gaps. Staying hydrated is equally important; water supports bodily functions and helps flush out toxins, thereby supporting immune health.

Mental well-being is intrinsically linked to physical health. Stress can compromise the immune system, making individuals more susceptible to illness. Incorporate relaxation and stress-reduction techniques into your routine, such as meditation, deep breathing exercises, or engaging in hobbies. Encourage open communication within the household to address concerns and provide mutual support, fostering a positive and resilient environment.

# Personal Hygiene in Prolonged Emergencies

When faced with prolonged emergencies, maintaining personal hygiene transcends mere comfort; it becomes crucial for health and morale. In situations where resources are limited and normal routines disrupted, personal hygiene can easily be overlooked, yet it remains a cornerstone of preventing illness and sustaining a semblance of normalcy. By preparing and adapting, you can ensure personal cleanliness and health, even in challenging conditions.

Water conservation becomes paramount during prolonged emergencies, where access may be restricted. Prioritize essential hygiene tasks such as handwashing, oral care, and face cleansing. Hand hygiene is your first line of defense against infectious diseases. In the absence of running water, utilize hand sanitizers with at least 60% alcohol for effective disinfection. Collect rainwater or greywater for non-drinking purposes and consider setting up a simple rainwater collection system to supplement limited supplies.

Bathing can be adapted to suit water scarcity. Sponge baths using a damp cloth and a small amount of water are effective for maintaining cleanliness. Focus on key areas prone to bacteria build-up, such as underarms, groin, and feet. Baby wipes or no-rinse bathing wipes are alternatives that can offer a refreshing cleanse when water resources are unavailable. Regularly change clothes and underwear to reduce bacteria and odor. If laundry facilities are inaccessible, hand wash garments using a minimal amount of water and biodegradable soap, and line dry to prevent mildew.

Oral hygiene should never be neglected, as dental issues can rapidly escalate into serious health problems. Brush your teeth at least twice a day using a small amount of water and toothpaste. If toothpaste is unavailable, substitute with baking soda or salt. Flossing is equally important to remove debris and prevent plaque buildup. Maintain a supply of dental hygiene products, and consider waterless alternatives such as chewable toothpaste tablets.

Hair care might seem less critical, but it plays a role in overall hygiene and comfort. Use dry shampoo or cornstarch to absorb excess oils and keep hair feeling fresh between washes. Braiding long hair can minimize tangles and dirt accumulation. When washing is possible, use a small basin to wet and rinse hair, conserving water as much as possible. Regularly brush hair to stimulate the scalp and distribute natural oils, promoting a healthier appearance.

Feminine hygiene requires careful planning and consideration. Stock a variety of menstrual products, such as pads, tampons, or menstrual cups, based on personal preference and availability. Menstrual cups offer a reusable option, reducing waste and the need for a large stockpile. Ensure access to clean water and soap for washing reusable products and maintaining personal cleanliness. Store supplies in a waterproof container to protect them from contamination.

Nail care is often overlooked but is vital for preventing infections. Keep nails trimmed and clean, as dirt and germs can accumulate beneath them. Avoid biting nails or picking at cuticles, as this can create entry points for bacteria. Use a nail brush for thorough cleaning, and maintain a basic manicure kit for trimming and filing.

Maintaining a hygienic environment also involves controlling body odor, which can impact morale and social interactions. Apply deodorant daily, or use natural alternatives like baking soda to neutralize odor. Regularly airing out and sun-drying clothing can also help eliminate smells and bacteria. Incorporate essential oils into your hygiene routine for a pleasant scent and potential antimicrobial benefits.

Psychological well-being is closely linked to personal hygiene. Feeling clean and presentable can boost confidence and reduce stress in uncertain times. Establish a daily routine that incorporates hygiene practices, providing structure and a sense of normalcy. Encourage household members to follow similar routines, fostering a collective commitment to cleanliness and health.

## Creating a Sanitation Plan

Creating a sanitation plan is an essential component of home security and resilience, particularly when preparing for scenarios where external support might be limited or unavailable. A well-structured sanitation plan not only ensures a clean and healthy living environment but also mitigates the risk of disease, contributing to the overall safety and peace of mind of your household. By developing a comprehensive approach to sanitation, you can manage waste effectively, maintain personal hygiene, and address the challenges posed by prolonged emergencies.

Begin by assessing your current sanitation infrastructure and identifying potential vulnerabilities. Consider the systems you rely on for waste disposal, water supply, and personal hygiene, and evaluate their capacity to function during disruptions. This assessment will help you prioritize areas that require reinforcement or alternative solutions, ensuring that you are prepared for a variety of scenarios.

Water is a critical resource in any sanitation plan, as it underpins both hygiene and waste management efforts. Establish a reliable water supply by storing potable water sufficient for at least two weeks, accounting for each household member's daily needs. Rainwater harvesting systems and water filtration devices can supplement your supply, providing additional resources for non-potable uses such as cleaning and flushing toilets. Regularly rotate stored water to maintain freshness and potability.

Personal hygiene is a cornerstone of a sanitation plan, as it directly impacts health and well-being. Stock up on essential hygiene products such as soap, toothpaste, toilet paper, and feminine hygiene items, ensuring that you have enough to last through extended periods of isolation. Explore alternative hygiene methods, such as dry shampoo and reusable menstrual products, to reduce dependency on limited resources. Develop a hygiene routine that can be adapted to varying water availability, prioritizing key practices like handwashing and oral care.

Waste management is another critical aspect of sanitation planning. In the absence of regular waste collection services, you will need to implement alternative disposal methods to prevent the accumulation of waste and the associated health risks. Composting is an effective way to manage organic waste, reducing landfill contributions and creating valuable fertilizer for gardening. Establish a composting system tailored to your space and needs, and educate household members on proper composting practices.

For inorganic waste, such as plastics and metals, recycling or repurposing materials can minimize environmental impact. Create a sorting system to separate recyclables from general waste, and research local facilities that accept these items. In situations where recycling is not feasible, consider reusing materials for DIY projects or storage solutions, extending their usefulness and reducing waste. waste disposal presents a unique challenge during prolonged emergencies, particularly if plumbing systems are compromised. Portable toilets or composting toilets can provide a viable solution, ensuring safe and sanitary waste management. These systems should be equipped with appropriate disposal materials, such as biodegradable bags or sawdust, to control odors and facilitate decomposition. Establish protocols for the safe handling and disposal of human waste, prioritizing hygiene and environmental protection.

Cleaning and disinfection are integral to maintaining a sanitary environment. Stock up on cleaning supplies, including multipurpose cleaners, disinfectants, and personal protective equipment like gloves and masks. Focus on high-touch surfaces and shared spaces, and establish a regular cleaning schedule to prevent the buildup of dirt and germs. When supplies are limited, explore natural cleaning alternatives like vinegar and baking soda, which can serve as effective substitutes for commercial products.

# Environmental Considerations

Understanding and incorporating environmental considerations into your sanitation and hygiene practices is crucial for creating a sustainable and resilient home. As you strive to protect your home and family, it's important to do so in a way that minimizes environmental impact. This not only preserves your immediate surroundings but also contributes to the broader goal of environmental stewardship, ensuring that resources are used wisely and responsibly.

Begin by evaluating your current sanitation practices and their environmental footprint. Consider the products you use for cleaning and personal hygiene, the waste you generate, and the resources you consume. Opt for eco-friendly alternatives where possible, such as biodegradable cleaning agents and personal care products that are free from harmful chemicals. These choices reduce the release of pollutants into the environment and protect your household from potential exposure to toxins.

Waste reduction is a key aspect of environmentally conscious sanitation. Implement strategies to minimize waste production, such as choosing products with minimal packaging or bulk purchasing to reduce overall packaging waste. Composting organic waste not only diverts it from landfills but also enriches soil health, promoting a sustainable cycle of nutrient reuse. By turning food scraps and yard waste into compost, you create a valuable resource for gardening while reducing your environmental impact.

Recycling plays a significant role in managing inorganic waste sustainably. Set up a comprehensive recycling system within your home, ensuring that materials like paper, plastics, glass, and metals are sorted and prepared for recycling facilities. Stay informed about local recycling guidelines to ensure compliance and maximize the effectiveness of your efforts. Additionally, look for ways to repurpose or upcycle items, giving them a new lease on life and further reducing waste.

Water conservation is another critical factor in environmentally sound sanitation practices. With water being an essential resource for hygiene and cleaning, it's imperative to use it judiciously. Install low-flow fixtures in bathrooms and kitchens to reduce water consumption without sacrificing performance. Collect rainwater for non-potable uses, such as irrigation and toilet flushing, to supplement your water supply and decrease reliance on municipal sources. Greywater systems can also be implemented to recycle water from sinks and showers for safe reuse in landscaping.

Energy-efficient appliances and practices contribute to environmental sustainability within your sanitation routine. Utilize energy-efficient washing machines and dishwashers, which consume less water and electricity, reducing your overall environmental footprint. When using appliances, run full loads to maximize efficiency, and select the appropriate settings for energy conservation.

Engaging in environmentally friendly pest management is crucial to maintaining hygiene without harming the ecosystem. Avoid chemical pesticides and opt for natural deterrents and traps that target pests without endangering beneficial wildlife or contaminating soil and water. Maintaining cleanliness and sealing entry points are effective preventive measures that reduce the need for chemical intervention.

Effective environmental sanitation also involves community efforts. Encourage neighborhood initiatives that focus on collective waste reduction, recycling, and resource sharing. Participate in local clean-up events and educational programs that promote sustainable practices, fostering a sense of community responsibility and cooperation. By working together, communities can achieve greater impact and resilience against environmental challenges.

Education and awareness are vital for integrating environmental considerations into your sanitation plan. Stay informed about developments in sustainable practices and technologies, and share this knowledge with your household. Encourage open discussions about the importance of environmental stewardship and the role each individual plays in reducing their ecological footprint. Conduct family workshops or activities that focus on sustainability, such as building a compost bin or creating reusable shopping bags.

# CHAPTER 11

# DEVELOPING MENTAL AND EMOTIONAL RESILIENCE

## Building a Resilient Mindset

Building a resilient mindset is a transformative endeavor, one that equips individuals to navigate life's challenges with confidence and tenacity. This process involves cultivating mental strength, emotional intelligence, and adaptive strategies to face adversity head-on. By developing these attributes, you not only enhance your ability to withstand stress but also empower yourself to thrive in the face of uncertainty.

The foundation of a resilient mindset lies in self-awareness. Understanding your thoughts, emotions, and reactions is crucial for managing them effectively. Take time to reflect on your experiences and identify patterns in your behavior. Journaling can be a powerful tool for this purpose, allowing you to process emotions and gain insight into your mental processes. By acknowledging your strengths and weaknesses, you can devise strategies to build on the former and address the latter, fostering a balanced and grounded perspective.

Emotional regulation is another key component of resilience. Life's unpredictability can trigger a wide range of emotions, from frustration to fear. Developing the ability to manage these emotions constructively is essential for maintaining mental equilibrium. Techniques such as mindfulness and meditation can help you cultivate a sense of calm and presence, enabling you to respond to stressors with clarity rather than impulsivity. Practice deep breathing exercises to center yourself in moments of tension, and explore visualization techniques that promote relaxation and positive thinking.

Cognitive flexibility, the ability to adapt your thinking in response to changing circumstances, is vital for resilience. Embrace a growth mindset, viewing challenges as opportunities for learning and development rather than insurmountable obstacles. By reframing setbacks as valuable experiences, you can maintain motivation and perseverance. Engage in activities that stimulate creative thinking and problem-solving, such as puzzles or brainstorming sessions, to enhance your cognitive agility.

Social support networks play a crucial role in fostering resilience. Surround yourself with individuals who uplift and encourage you, providing a sense of belonging and security. Cultivate meaningful relationships by engaging in open and honest communication, sharing your thoughts and feelings with trusted friends or family members. Participate in community groups or support networks that align with your interests and values, creating connections that reinforce your resilience.

Adopting healthy coping mechanisms is essential for managing stress effectively. Identify activities that bring you joy and relaxation, such as exercise, reading, or creative pursuits, and incorporate them into your routine. Recognize the importance of self-care, prioritizing activities that nurture your physical and emotional well-being. Avoid maladaptive coping strategies, such as substance abuse or avoidance, which can undermine your resilience and exacerbate stress.

Developing problem-solving skills is a practical approach to building resilience. Break challenges into manageable steps, and create action plans to address them systematically. Practice critical thinking by evaluating potential solutions and considering their outcomes. When faced with uncertainty, focus on aspects within your control and take proactive steps to influence them positively. By approaching problems with a solution-oriented mindset, you enhance your confidence and ability to navigate adversity.

Optimism, the belief in positive outcomes, is a hallmark of resilient individuals. Cultivate an optimistic outlook by focusing on gratitude and celebrating small victories. Keep a gratitude journal to record daily highlights, reinforcing a positive perspective. While optimism doesn't negate the reality of challenges, it provides a hopeful lens through which to view them, bolstering your motivation and perseverance.

Building resilience also involves setting realistic goals and expectations. Define clear objectives that align with your values and aspirations, breaking them down into achievable milestones. Celebrate progress along the way, acknowledging your efforts and achievements. Avoid perfectionism, recognizing that setbacks and mistakes are natural components of the growth process. By maintaining a balanced and realistic approach, you can sustain momentum and motivation.

Finally, resilience is not a destination but a journey. It requires ongoing commitment and effort, evolving as you encounter new experiences and challenges. Embrace a mindset of lifelong learning, continuously seeking opportunities to grow and develop. Reflect on your progress regularly, and adjust your strategies as needed to sustain your resilience.

In cultivating a resilient mindset, you empower yourself to face life's uncertainties with strength and grace. By embracing self-awareness, emotional regulation, cognitive flexibility, and social support, you create a foundation of resilience that supports your mental and emotional well-being. Through dedication and practice, you can navigate adversity with confidence and emerge from challenges not only intact but transformed, ready to embrace the possibilities of the future.

## Coping with Stress and Isolation

In life's journey, especially during periods of challenge and change, stress and isolation can feel like relentless companions. They test our resilience, stretching emotional reserves and demanding fortitude in the face of hardship. Yet, even in these moments, there lies an opportunity for growth, a chance to harness resilience, and emerge stronger. Understanding how to cope effectively with these forces is essential, not only for survival but for thriving in all seasons of life.

To begin, it is crucial to acknowledge that stress and isolation are universal experiences. They are not merely byproducts of difficult times but can serve as catalysts for growth and transformation. The key lies in how we respond to them. Cultivating resilience does not mean avoiding challenges but rather developing the skills to navigate them. It is about flexibility, adaptability, and the courage to face adversity head-on.

Acknowledge that stress is a natural response, an instinctive reaction to perceived threats. It is the body's alarm system, signaling that something requires attention. While stress can be a powerful motivator, chronic stress, if left unchecked, can take a toll on mental and physical health. Recognizing stressors and understanding how they manifest in your life is the first step towards managing them. This awareness allows you to take control, rather than being swept along by the currents of stress.

A cornerstone of managing stress lies in effective coping mechanisms. These are the tools that enable you to navigate life's challenges with resilience. Engage in activities that promote relaxation and well-being, such as yoga, meditation, or deep-breathing exercises. These practices counteract stress, calming the mind and soothing the body. Embrace the power of mindfulness, grounding yourself in the present moment. Techniques such as deep breathing or meditation can provide clarity, helping you to navigate complex emotions and stressors with greater ease.

Stress management is not merely about reducing tension but also about fostering resilience. Incorporate practices that promote well-being, such as physical activity, healthy eating, and regular sleep. Exercise, in particular, is a powerful stress-reliever, releasing endorphins and boosting mood. Prioritize activities that nourish the soul, whether it be painting, reading, or spending time in nature. Acknowledge the importance of self-care, recognizing that it is not an indulgence but a necessity.

Social support is a vital component of resilience. During challenging times, it can be a lifeline, offering comfort and perspective. Foster connections with loved ones, even when physically apart. In an age of technology, distance need not equate to separation. Reach out, share experiences, and offer support. Remember that connection is a two-way street; be open to receiving and giving in equal measure.

Equally important is fostering a resilient mindset. Embrace change and uncertainty as opportunities for growth. Challenges, while daunting, are an invitation to learn and evolve. Cultivate resilience by maintaining a positive outlook, even in difficult times. Acknowledge that while you cannot control every circumstance, you can choose your response. Embrace change as an opportunity for growth, and trust in your capacity to overcome adversity.

Resilience is also about adaptability. In a world of constant change, the ability to adapt is a powerful tool. Embrace flexibility, be open to new possibilities, and willing to adjust. Remember that resilience is not about avoiding challenges but about overcoming them. It is the ability to face adversity with courage, adapt, and grow stronger.

# Supporting Family Members Emotionally

Supporting family members emotionally is a vital aspect of fostering a resilient and harmonious home environment. It requires empathy, communication, and an understanding of the unique dynamics and needs of each family member. By creating a supportive atmosphere, you not only help your loved ones navigate their challenges but also strengthen the bonds that hold your family together.

Begin by actively listening to your family members. Listening is more than just hearing words; it's about understanding the feelings and concerns behind them. When someone shares their thoughts or emotions, offer your full attention, free from distractions. Make eye contact, nod, and offer verbal affirmations to show that you are engaged. Reflect back what you hear to ensure clarity and demonstrate empathy. By creating a safe space for dialogue, you encourage openness and vulnerability, which are essential for emotional support.

Effective communication goes hand in hand with listening. Express your thoughts and feelings clearly and respectfully, avoiding blame or judgment. Use "I" statements to convey your perspective without making the other person feel defensive. For example, instead of saying "You never listen to me," try "I feel unheard when I share my thoughts." This approach fosters constructive conversations and encourages mutual understanding.

Recognize that each family member may have different emotional needs. Some may require reassurance, while others may benefit from practical support or space to process their feelings. Tailor your approach to suit the individual's personality and preferences. Be patient and flexible, understanding that emotions can be complex and may not always be easily articulated.

Offer validation and encouragement. Let your family members know that their feelings are valid and that it's okay to experience a range of emotions. Avoid dismissing or minimizing their concerns, even if they seem trivial to you. Instead, offer words of support and encouragement, reinforcing their strengths and resilience. For instance, if a family member is anxious about a new job, acknowledge their nerves but also highlight their skills and past successes.

Create opportunities for quality time together. Shared activities, whether it's a family dinner, a game night, or a walk in the park, provide a chance to connect and strengthen relationships. These moments foster a sense of belonging and support, reminding family members that they are not alone in their struggles. Additionally, shared experiences can create positive memories that contribute to the family's emotional well-being.

Promote healthy coping mechanisms within the family. Encourage activities that reduce stress and promote well-being, such as exercise, hobbies, or relaxation techniques. Lead by example, demonstrating the importance of self-care and balance. Encourage family members to express their emotions through creative outlets like art, music, or writing. These activities can serve as a release valve for pent-up emotions and provide a sense of accomplishment and joy.

Foster an environment of trust and openness. Be consistent in your actions and words, showing reliability and integrity. Respect each family member's privacy and confidentiality, especially when they share sensitive information. This trust is the bedrock of emotional support, allowing family members to feel safe in being vulnerable and honest with each other.

Recognize the signs of emotional distress and offer help. Changes in behavior, mood swings, withdrawal, or a loss of interest in activities may indicate that a family member is struggling. Approach them with care and concern, expressing your willingness to support them. Encourage them to seek professional help if needed, reassuring them that there is no shame in seeking assistance. Offer to help them find resources or accompany them to appointments if they are comfortable with it.

Encourage individual resilience within the family. While providing support is crucial, it's also important to empower family members to develop their own coping strategies. Encourage problem-solving, critical thinking, and self-reflection. Celebrate their achievements and progress, fostering a sense of autonomy and confidence. By helping family members build their own resilience, you equip them with the tools to face future challenges independently.

Be mindful of your own emotional well-being as you support others. It's easy to become overwhelmed or emotionally drained when focusing on the needs of others. Practice self-care, set boundaries when necessary, and seek support from friends, support groups, or professionals if needed. Remember that taking care of yourself enables you to be a more effective support for your family.

## Utilizing Relaxation and Meditation Techniques

The modern world, with its relentless pace and constant noise, often leaves individuals feeling overwhelmed and stressed. To navigate this whirlwind, the cultivation of mental and emotional resilience becomes a necessary endeavor. Central to this pursuit is the effective use of relaxation and meditation techniques. These practices are not just temporary escapes but powerful tools that enhance resilience, allowing one to face life's challenges with a calm, centered mind.

At the heart of relaxation techniques lies the principle of intentional slowing down. It's about creating a mental space where stress is not in control. Deep breathing is one such foundational practice. By focusing on each breath, inhaling deeply through the nose and exhaling slowly through the mouth, one can activate the body's relaxation response. This simple yet effective technique reduces heart rate, lowers blood pressure, and induces a sense of calm. The beauty of deep breathing is its accessibility; it can be practiced anywhere, anytime, offering immediate respite from stress.

Progressive muscle relaxation is another technique that harnesses the mind-body connection. This method involves systematically tensing and then relaxing different muscle groups in the body. Start from the toes and work upwards, or vice versa, focusing on each muscle group for a few seconds. This practice not only relieves physical tension but also heightens awareness of where stress manifests in the body. By releasing these tensions, a deep state of relaxation and a sense of control over one's physical state are achieved.

Guided imagery is a technique that employs the power of visualization. By imagining a peaceful scene or a place where one feels safe and relaxed, the mind is transported away from stressors. This mental escape can be facilitated by audio recordings or personal scripts. The key is to engage all senses in the visualization, noticing the colors, sounds, and feelings associated with the imagined environment. This technique fosters a sense of peace and tranquility, even amidst chaos.

Meditation, a practice with roots in ancient traditions, offers profound benefits for mental and emotional resilience. Mindfulness meditation, in particular, focuses on cultivating present-moment awareness. By observing thoughts and feelings without judgment, mindfulness fosters a deep sense of acceptance and clarity. This practice involves setting aside time each day to sit quietly, focusing on the breath or a mantra. As thoughts arise, they are acknowledged and released, gently returning attention to the present moment. Over time, mindfulness meditation enhances emotional regulation, reducing reactivity to stressors.

Loving-kindness meditation is another form of practice that extends compassion towards oneself and others. This meditation involves silently repeating phrases of goodwill and kindness, initially directed towards oneself and gradually extended to others, including those with whom one may have difficulties. By cultivating compassion and empathy, loving-kindness meditation builds emotional resilience, breaking down barriers and fostering connection.

Transcendental meditation, a form of silent mantra meditation, involves silently repeating a specific word or phrase to settle the mind into a state of restful awareness. Practitioners of transcendental meditation often report reduced anxiety and improved emotional stability, as the practice allows the mind to transcend active thought processes, accessing a deeper state of consciousness.

Incorporating these techniques into daily life requires commitment and consistency. Establishing a regular practice routine, even if it begins with just a few minutes each day, is crucial. Designate a specific time and space for practice, free from distractions. Whether it's a corner of a room or a spot in a garden, having a dedicated space reinforces the habit and signals to the mind that it's time to unwind.

It's important to approach these practices with patience and kindness towards oneself. The benefits of relaxation and meditation are cumulative, building over time. Some days may feel more challenging than others, and that's perfectly normal. The key is to maintain the practice, trusting in its long-term benefits.

For those new to meditation, guided sessions can be beneficial. Numerous apps and online resources offer guided meditations of varying lengths and focuses, providing structure and support for beginners. These resources can be particularly helpful in navigating initial challenges and building confidence in one's practice.

Beyond individual practice, consider engaging in group sessions or classes. The communal aspect of meditation and relaxation can enhance motivation and provide a sense of shared experience. Many communities offer meditation groups, yoga classes, or wellness workshops that incorporate relaxation techniques.

## Resources for Mental Health Support

Navigating the complexities of life often requires more than inner strength and personal coping mechanisms. Accessing external resources for mental health support can be an invaluable component in developing mental and emotional resilience. These resources, ranging from professional services to community and online platforms, provide guidance, support, and tools that help individuals manage stress, anxiety, and other mental health challenges.

Professional mental health services are a cornerstone of effective support. Psychologists, psychiatrists, and licensed therapists offer a range of therapeutic approaches tailored to individual needs. Cognitive Behavioral Therapy (CBT), for instance, focuses on identifying and changing negative thought patterns and behaviors. Dialectical Behavior Therapy (DBT) is particularly effective for those dealing with intense emotions and is often used for mood disorders. Engaging in therapy provides a structured environment to explore emotions, identify triggers, and develop coping strategies.

Psychiatrists, being medical doctors, can offer additional support through medication management, particularly for those with conditions like depression, anxiety disorders, or bipolar disorder. Medication can help stabilize mood and alleviate symptoms, making it easier for individuals to engage in therapy and other resilience-building activities. It's essential to have open communication with healthcare providers to ensure that treatment plans are effective and adjusted as needed.

Support groups offer a community-based approach to mental health. These groups provide a safe space for individuals to share experiences, gain insights, and find solace in knowing they are not alone. Many support groups are focused on specific issues, such as grief, addiction, or chronic illness, allowing participants to connect with others facing similar challenges. Peer support fosters a sense of belonging and can be a powerful motivator in the journey towards resilience.

Online resources have become increasingly accessible, offering a wealth of information and support at one's fingertips. Websites, forums, and mobile applications provide educational materials, self-help tools, and virtual communities. Platforms like these offer anonymity, which can be particularly appealing for those hesitant to seek face-to-face support. Online therapy services have also gained prominence, providing flexible and convenient access to professional help. These services often include video sessions, messaging, and digital resources, making mental health support more accessible than ever before.

Community organizations and non-profits often offer mental health services and programs at little or no cost. These organizations may provide workshops, counseling, and crisis intervention services. Local community centers or health departments are excellent starting points for discovering available resources. Many of these organizations focus on underserved populations, ensuring that everyone, regardless of financial situation, has access to the support they need.

Educational institutions, from schools to universities, also play a crucial role in mental health support. School counselors, psychologists, and wellness programs provide resources and assistance to students navigating academic and personal challenges. These services are vital in promoting resilience among young people, equipping them with skills to manage stress and emotions effectively.

Workplace mental health programs are becoming more prevalent as employers recognize the importance of supporting their employees' well-being. Employee Assistance Programs (EAPs) often include counseling services, workshops, and wellness initiatives. By utilizing these programs, individuals can access support within their professional environment, promoting a healthy work-life balance and reducing burnout.

For those in crisis, hotlines and emergency services provide immediate support. Trained counselors are available 24/7 to offer guidance, support, and intervention. Whether it's a mental health crisis or the need for someone to talk to, these services are a critical lifeline. It's important to have these numbers readily available and not hesitate to reach out when in need.

Incorporating these resources into one's life requires a proactive approach. Begin by identifying the type of support that aligns with personal needs and preferences. Consider factors such as the nature of the challenge, availability, and comfort level with various forms of support. Establishing a network of resources, including professional help, peer support, and self-help tools, creates a comprehensive support system.

It's important to approach mental health support with an open mind and a willingness to explore different options. What works for one person may not work for another, and that's perfectly acceptable. The journey to resilience is unique for each individual, and finding the right combination of resources is an integral part of that journey.

# CHAPTER 12

# BUILDING COMMUNITY AND NEIGHBORHOOD NETWORKS

## Establishing Trust and Cooperation

Building strong community and neighborhood networks is an essential aspect of achieving unbreakable security and peace of mind. Establishing trust and cooperation among neighbors creates a collective resilience that benefits everyone involved. In an age where social connections can be fragmented, reimagining the neighborhood as a bastion of mutual support and shared responsibility is both a practical and rewarding endeavor.

The foundation of any robust neighborhood network lies in trust. Trust is not built overnight; it requires consistent, genuine interactions and a shared vision for a secure and harmonious community. Begin by getting to know your neighbors. Organize informal gatherings such as barbecues, potlucks, or block parties. These events provide an opportunity for neighbors to connect, share stories, and build rapport in a relaxed setting. As relationships form, a sense of camaraderie and mutual respect naturally develops, paving the way for deeper collaboration.

Communication is a vital component of trust-building. Establish open lines of communication through both traditional and digital means. Consider creating a neighborhood newsletter or bulletin board to share important updates, safety tips, and community events. Digital platforms like neighborhood-specific social media groups or messaging apps can facilitate real-time communication and coordination. Encourage transparency and inclusivity in these communications, ensuring that all voices are heard and valued.

Cooperation among neighbors is most effective when there is a shared commitment to collective goals. Engage the community in discussions about common concerns and aspirations. Whether it's enhancing neighborhood safety, organizing community clean-ups, or planning social events, involving everyone in the decision-making process fosters a sense of ownership and investment. Forming committees or working groups can help organize efforts and distribute responsibilities, ensuring that initiatives are sustainable and inclusive.

Safety is often a top priority for neighborhoods, and cooperation plays a crucial role in enhancing security. Establishing a neighborhood watch program is a practical way to formalize collective vigilance. These programs encourage neighbors to look out for one another, report suspicious activities, and work together to deter crime. Training sessions or workshops on topics like emergency preparedness, first aid, and home security can further empower residents with the skills and knowledge needed to protect themselves and their community.

Resource sharing is another powerful aspect of neighborhood cooperation. By pooling resources, such as tools, equipment, or expertise, neighbors can achieve more than they could individually. Creating a shared inventory or lending library can facilitate this exchange, reducing individual costs and fostering a spirit of generosity. In times of crisis or emergency, resource-sharing becomes even more critical, ensuring that all community members have access to essential supplies and support.

Fostering a culture of mutual aid and support extends beyond material resources. Emotional support and companionship are equally important in building resilient communities. Encourage neighbors to check in on one another, especially those who may be vulnerable or isolated. Simple gestures, like offering assistance with errands or providing a listening ear, can make a significant difference in someone's well-being. Building a network of support strengthens the emotional fabric of the community, making it more resilient to both everyday challenges and larger crises.

Conflict resolution is an inevitable part of community life, and handling disagreements constructively is crucial for maintaining trust and cooperation. Establish clear and fair processes for addressing disputes, whether through mediation, community meetings, or consensus-building exercises. Encourage open dialogue, active listening, and empathy, aiming to find solutions that respect everyone's needs and perspectives. By addressing conflicts head-on, rather than allowing them to fester, the community can maintain harmony and cohesion.

Engaging in community preparedness initiatives is another avenue for strengthening neighborhood networks. Collaborate on disaster preparedness plans, ensuring that everyone knows what to do in case of emergencies such as natural disasters or power outages. Conduct regular drills and simulations to practice these plans, building confidence and competence among residents. Preparedness initiatives not only enhance safety but also reinforce the sense of community and shared responsibility.

To sustain trust and cooperation, celebrate the community's achievements and milestones. Recognize the contributions of individuals and groups, expressing gratitude for their efforts. Organize events or ceremonies that honor the community's successes, whether it's completing a project, achieving a safety milestone, or simply enjoying a year of harmonious living. Celebrations not only boost morale but also strengthen bonds, reminding everyone of the value and rewards of working together.

Ultimately, establishing trust and cooperation in a neighborhood is about creating a sense of belonging and shared purpose. It requires ongoing effort, patience, and a willingness to engage with others in meaningful ways. By investing in these relationships, neighbors not only enhance their collective security but also enrich their lives with the connections and support that a vibrant community offers. In a world where self-reliance is often emphasized, rediscovering the power of community and cooperation opens up new possibilities for security, resilience, and peace of mind.

# Resource Sharing and Mutual Aid

Resource sharing and mutual aid are foundational pillars of a thriving community, fostering cooperation and resilience in times of both stability and crisis. These practices draw on the strengths and capabilities of individuals, creating a network of support that amplifies collective security and well-being. As we look to strengthen our neighborhoods, understanding and implementing effective resource-sharing strategies can transform a collection of individuals into a cohesive and supportive community.

At the heart of resource sharing is the idea that pooling resources—whether they be material, skills, or information—can achieve more than isolated efforts. It begins with recognizing the assets already present within the community. Every resident possesses unique skills and knowledge, from gardening and carpentry to technology and teaching. Encouraging neighbors to share their skills not only benefits others but also fosters a sense of belonging and purpose. Setting up workshops or skill-sharing events can be a practical starting point, offering opportunities for residents to learn from each other and contribute their expertise.

Material resources are another crucial aspect of mutual aid. Many items, such as tools, equipment, and appliances, are used infrequently, making them ideal candidates for sharing. Establishing a communal inventory or lending library allows residents to borrow what they need without the expense of purchasing new items. This approach not only saves money but also reduces waste and promotes sustainable living. For example, a community tool shed could house everything from power drills to gardening supplies, accessible to all who contribute to its upkeep.

In addition to physical resources, information sharing is a powerful component of mutual aid. Neighborhood networks can facilitate the exchange of valuable information on topics such as local services, safety tips, or emergency preparedness. Creating a community newsletter, website, or social media group can serve as a hub for disseminating this information. It's important to ensure that these channels are inclusive and accessible to everyone, taking into account diverse communication preferences and needs.

Resource sharing extends into times of crisis, where mutual aid becomes a lifeline. Natural disasters, economic downturns, or personal emergencies can strain individual resources, making community support vital. Establishing an emergency fund or resource pool can provide immediate assistance to those in need, whether it's through financial support, food supplies, or temporary housing. Community members can contribute according to their means, creating a safety net that enhances resilience and solidarity.

Food sharing is another meaningful way to support each other. Community gardens or shared plots can provide fresh produce, while food co-ops or meal-sharing programs can ensure that everyone has access to nutritious meals. These initiatives not only address food security but also strengthen social bonds as neighbors work together towards a common goal.

Mutual aid also encompasses emotional and social support. Building a community culture where residents feel comfortable reaching out for help is crucial. Encourage neighbors to check in on each other, especially those who may be vulnerable or isolated. Simple acts of kindness, such as running errands for an elderly neighbor or offering a listening ear, can foster a supportive and caring environment.

To implement successful resource-sharing and mutual aid systems, it is essential to establish clear guidelines and expectations. Create a framework that outlines how resources are shared, responsibilities are divided, and contributions are recognized. This framework should be flexible, allowing for adjustments as the community's needs and dynamics evolve.

Engaging in regular community meetings or forums can facilitate open dialogue and collective decision-making. These gatherings provide a platform for residents to express their needs, propose ideas, and resolve any issues that arise. By involving everyone in the process, mutual aid initiatives are more likely to be embraced and sustained.

Trust is the bedrock of effective resource sharing and mutual aid. Building trust requires transparency, accountability, and a commitment to honoring agreements. Encourage open communication and address any concerns promptly to maintain a positive and collaborative atmosphere. Recognizing and celebrating contributions, whether big or small, can reinforce a sense of community pride and belonging.

# Coordinating Neighborhood Surveillance

Effective neighborhood surveillance is a cornerstone of community safety, acting as both a deterrent to potential threats and a means of rapid response in emergencies. Coordinating such efforts requires a blend of organization, technology, and the goodwill of community members. By establishing a structured surveillance network, neighborhoods can significantly enhance their security and foster a collective sense of safety and peace.

The first step in coordinating neighborhood surveillance is to establish a core group of dedicated volunteers. These individuals will serve as the coordinators and point of contact for the surveillance initiative. It's crucial that they represent a cross-section of the community, ensuring diverse perspectives and widespread buy-in. Begin by hosting a community meeting to discuss the concept, gauge interest, and identify potential volunteers. Transparency and inclusivity at this stage lay the groundwork for a cohesive effort.

Once the core group is established, the next step is to conduct a comprehensive assessment of the neighborhood's surveillance needs. This involves identifying high-risk areas, such as poorly lit streets, secluded alleys, or entry points to the community. Engaging residents in this assessment can provide valuable insights and foster a sense of shared responsibility. Residents often know their areas best, and their input will be invaluable in identifying vulnerabilities.

With the assessment complete, the group can move on to designing the surveillance strategy. This plan should outline the types of surveillance measures to be implemented, such as the installation of security cameras, neighborhood patrols, or the use of motion sensor lighting. It's essential to balance the need for security with privacy considerations, ensuring that surveillance measures are respectful of residents' rights and legal requirements. Involving a legal advisor or consulting local law enforcement can help navigate potential legal pitfalls.

Technology plays a pivotal role in modern surveillance efforts. Selecting the right equipment is critical, and the options are vast. Surveillance cameras should offer high resolution and night vision capabilities to be effective. Wireless cameras allow for greater flexibility in placement and can be easily integrated into a network. Consider setting up a centralized monitoring system where footage from various cameras can be accessed and reviewed in real-time. This system can be managed by the core group or a designated security company, depending on the community's resources and preferences.

Neighborhood patrols, whether conducted on foot, by bicycle, or by car, add an active layer to the surveillance network. Volunteers can take turns patrolling the area, watching for unusual activity and serving as a visible deterrent to potential wrongdoers. It's important to provide basic training to these volunteers, covering observation techniques, communication protocols, and personal safety measures. Establishing a direct line of communication with local law enforcement ensures that any incidents are promptly reported and addressed.

Communication is key to the success of a neighborhood surveillance network. Creating a dedicated communication channel, such as a messaging app or email list, allows for the rapid sharing of information among residents. This channel can be used to report suspicious activities, share safety tips, and coordinate patrol schedules. It's vital that all participants adhere to agreed-upon protocols, maintaining the confidentiality and accuracy of shared information.

Regular meetings and updates keep the surveillance network engaged and informed. These gatherings provide an opportunity to review the effectiveness of current measures, discuss any challenges, and make necessary adjustments. Involving the broader community in these meetings can help sustain interest and support for the initiative. Recognizing and celebrating successes, such as a reduction in crime rates or successful intervention in a potential incident, reinforces the value of the surveillance network.

To enhance the effectiveness of neighborhood surveillance, consider integrating it with other community safety initiatives. Collaborating with local authorities, neighborhood associations, and nearby communities can expand the reach and impact of the efforts. Joint initiatives, such as safety workshops or crime prevention seminars, can further educate residents and strengthen community ties.

# Engaging in Community Preparedness Initiatives

Community preparedness initiatives are vital in fostering resilience and ensuring that neighborhoods are well-equipped to face emergencies and adversities. These initiatives promote collaboration, enhance safety, and build a sense of unity among residents. By engaging in collective preparedness efforts, communities can mitigate the impact of disasters, improve their response capabilities, and strengthen social bonds.

The first step in engaging in community preparedness is raising awareness and educating residents about potential risks. Organize informational sessions or workshops to discuss common threats such as natural disasters, power outages, or health emergencies. These gatherings serve as a platform to share knowledge, dispel myths, and encourage proactive planning. Inviting experts, such as emergency responders or disaster management professionals, to speak at these events can provide valuable insights and lend credibility to the initiative.

Building a culture of preparedness requires involving all segments of the community. Tailor outreach efforts to engage diverse groups, including families, seniors, and individuals with disabilities. By addressing the unique needs and concerns of different populations, preparedness initiatives become more inclusive and effective. Establishing a network of community leaders or ambassadors can help facilitate communication and mobilize residents, ensuring that everyone is informed and involved.

Developing a comprehensive community emergency plan is a cornerstone of preparedness. This plan should outline procedures for communication, evacuation, sheltering, and resource distribution during emergencies. Collaborate with local authorities, emergency services, and neighboring communities to create a cohesive and coordinated response strategy. Ensure that the plan is easily accessible and well-communicated to all residents, using multiple channels such as printed materials, digital platforms, and community meetings.

Regular drills and simulations are essential for testing the effectiveness of emergency plans and building residents' confidence in their ability to respond. Organize practice exercises that mimic real-life scenarios, such as fire evacuations, earthquake drills, or flood response. These simulations provide an opportunity to identify gaps in the plan, refine procedures, and reinforce the importance of preparedness. Encourage participation from all community members, emphasizing that practice is key to reducing panic and confusion during actual emergencies.

Resource management is a critical aspect of community preparedness. Establish a system for stockpiling essential supplies, including food, water, medical kits, and emergency equipment. Encourage residents to contribute to a communal stockpile or maintain their own emergency kits. Create a directory of local resources, such as shelters, medical facilities, and supply depots, to ensure that residents know where to turn for assistance. Collaborate with local businesses and organizations to secure support and partnerships that enhance resource availability.

Effective communication is vital during emergencies, and establishing reliable channels is a priority. Develop a communication plan that includes methods for disseminating information before, during, and after an emergency. Consider using a combination of traditional and modern communication tools, such as phone trees, text alerts, community radios, and social media. Ensure that communication is clear, timely, and accessible to all, taking into account language barriers and technological limitations.

Community preparedness initiatives thrive on collaboration and partnerships. Foster strong relationships with local government agencies, emergency services, non-profits, and neighboring communities. These partnerships provide access to expertise, resources, and support that can bolster the community's preparedness efforts. Engage in joint exercises or training programs to build trust and coordination among different entities, creating a unified front in the face of adversity.

Empowering residents with the skills and knowledge needed to respond to emergencies enhances the overall resilience of the community. Offer training programs on first aid, CPR, fire safety, and disaster response. Encourage residents to become certified in emergency management or volunteer with local response teams. By equipping individuals with practical skills, the community becomes more self-reliant and better prepared to handle unexpected challenges.

# Resolving Conflicts and Disagreements

Conflicts and disagreements are inevitable in any community. How they are managed can either strengthen or undermine the bonds that hold a neighborhood together. Addressing conflicts effectively is crucial for maintaining harmony and fostering a sense of belonging. It requires a thoughtful approach that emphasizes communication, empathy, and collaboration, transforming potential divides into opportunities for growth and understanding.

The first step in resolving conflicts is to create an environment where open communication is encouraged. Establishing regular community meetings or forums provides a platform for residents to voice their concerns and discuss issues openly. These gatherings should be designed to promote constructive dialogue, ensuring that all participants feel safe and respected. Set ground rules that encourage active listening, civility, and a focus on problem-solving.

It's important to recognize and acknowledge the emotions involved in conflicts. Emotions can run high, and addressing them is essential for finding resolution. Encourage individuals to express their feelings and perspectives without fear of judgment. Empathy plays a vital role here; by understanding the emotions and motivations of others, residents can find common ground and work towards mutually beneficial solutions.

Mediation is a valuable tool in conflict resolution, offering a neutral space where parties can come together to discuss their differences. A trained mediator, whether a community member or an external professional, can facilitate these discussions, helping to clarify issues and explore potential solutions. Mediation focuses on collaboration rather than confrontation, guiding participants toward agreements that are satisfactory to all parties involved.

When disagreements arise, it is crucial to focus on interests rather than positions. Positions are often rigid and can lead to impasse, whereas interests reveal the underlying needs and desires that drive conflict. By identifying shared interests, community members can develop creative solutions that address the root causes of disagreements. This approach fosters a spirit of cooperation and innovation, transforming conflicts into opportunities for positive change.

In some cases, conflict resolution may require compromise. Encourage residents to be flexible and willing to make concessions when necessary. Compromise does not mean sacrificing core values; rather, it involves finding a balance that respects the needs of all parties. Highlight the importance of mutual respect and the long-term benefits of maintaining positive relationships within the community.

Transparency is key to preventing misunderstandings and building trust. Ensure that decision-making processes are open and inclusive, allowing residents to participate and contribute. Share information about community initiatives, policies, and changes that may impact residents, keeping everyone informed and engaged. When people feel they have a voice and are kept in the loop, they are more likely to support community decisions and initiatives.

In situations where conflicts persist, it may be necessary to involve external support, such as local government officials or community organizations. These entities can provide additional resources, expertise, and impartiality, helping to facilitate resolution. Collaboration with external partners can also strengthen the community's capacity to manage future conflicts independently.

Education and training in conflict resolution skills can empower residents to handle disagreements effectively. Workshops or seminars on topics such as communication, negotiation, and mediation can equip individuals with the tools they need to navigate conflicts constructively. By building these skills within the community, residents become more confident and capable of addressing issues as they arise.

Celebrating successful conflict resolution reinforces the value of constructive dialogue and collaboration. Acknowledge the efforts of individuals and groups who contribute to resolving disagreements, highlighting the positive outcomes achieved. These celebrations can take the form of community events, public recognition, or simply expressions of gratitude. Recognizing achievements in conflict resolution inspires others to adopt similar approaches and strengthens the community's commitment to maintaining harmony.

# CHAPTER 13

# ADAPTING TO EVOLVING THREATS AND CONDITIONS

## Monitoring and Reacting to New Developments

Communities today face an ever-changing landscape of threats and conditions that require vigilance and adaptability. The ability to monitor and react to new developments is crucial for maintaining safety and resilience. As neighborhoods seek to protect themselves from various challenges, implementing effective strategies for staying informed and responsive becomes a vital component of community security.

Monitoring new developments begins with establishing reliable information channels. Residents must have access to accurate and timely information about emerging threats, whether they be natural disasters, public health crises, or changes in local crime patterns. Developing a network of trusted sources, including local government agencies, emergency services, and community organizations, ensures that residents receive credible updates. This network can include digital communications such as community websites, social media groups, and email alerts, as well as traditional methods like newsletters and bulletin boards.

To enhance the flow of information, consider appointing a community liaison or information officer. This individual or team can act as the primary point of contact for gathering, verifying, and disseminating information to the community. By centralizing this role, the community can reduce confusion and ensure a consistent message is communicated to all residents. This approach fosters trust and confidence in the information being shared, which is crucial during times of uncertainty.

Technology plays a pivotal role in monitoring new developments. Implementing surveillance and monitoring systems, such as security cameras and sensors, can provide real-time data on local conditions. These systems can be integrated into a larger network that includes weather alerts, traffic updates, and emergency notifications. By leveraging technology, communities can gain a comprehensive view of their environment, enabling them to detect potential threats and respond proactively.

Community engagement is a key aspect of effective monitoring. Encourage residents to report unusual activities or changes in their surroundings, fostering a sense of shared responsibility for neighborhood safety. Establishing a community watch program can formalize this engagement, providing a structure for residents to collaborate on monitoring efforts. Training sessions or workshops on observation techniques and reporting procedures can empower residents to contribute effectively to the community's monitoring efforts.

Reacting to new developments requires a flexible and adaptive approach. Communities should develop contingency plans that outline responses to various scenarios, ensuring that they can quickly adapt to changing conditions. These plans should be regularly reviewed and updated to reflect new information and lessons learned from past experiences. Involving residents in the planning process not only enhances the quality of the plans but also ensures that everyone is familiar with the procedures and their roles during an emergency.

Effective communication is crucial during the reaction phase. Clear and concise communication helps prevent misinformation and panic, providing residents with the guidance they need to take appropriate action. Establish multiple communication channels to ensure that all residents receive the information, regardless of their preferred methods. Regular updates, even when there is no new information, can reassure residents and maintain their confidence in the community's response efforts.

Flexibility and resourcefulness are essential traits for reacting to new developments. Encourage residents to think creatively and adaptively when faced with challenges, drawing on the diverse skills and experiences within the community. By fostering a culture of innovation, communities can develop unique solutions to problems and navigate complex situations effectively. This adaptability is particularly important in dynamic environments where conditions can change rapidly and unpredictably.

Partnerships with external organizations can enhance the community's capacity to react to new developments. Collaborate with local authorities, non-profits, and neighboring communities to access additional resources, expertise, and support. These partnerships can provide valuable insights and assistance, enabling the community to respond more effectively to evolving threats. Joint training exercises and simulations can strengthen these relationships and improve coordination during actual emergencies.

Evaluating the community's response to new developments is an important step in the learning process. After a situation has been addressed, conduct a debriefing session to review what worked well and what could be improved. Gather feedback from residents and stakeholders to identify areas for enhancement and celebrate successes. This reflective practice helps the community build on its strengths and address any weaknesses, ensuring that it is better prepared for future challenges.

## Updating Security Measures and Plans

Updating security measures and plans is a critical component in ensuring the safety and resilience of any community. In a rapidly changing world, threats can evolve quickly, and the systems put in place to protect us must be agile and responsive to these shifts. By regularly reviewing and enhancing security strategies, neighborhoods can remain vigilant against potential dangers, fostering an environment where residents feel secure and connected.

The process of updating security measures begins with a comprehensive assessment of current systems. This involves evaluating existing protocols, technology, and resources to determine their effectiveness in addressing contemporary threats. Engage with community members, local authorities, and security experts to gather a range of perspectives on areas that may require improvement. This collaborative approach ensures that updates are well-informed and reflect the diverse needs of the community.

Technology is a significant factor in modern security measures. As advancements continue to emerge, integrating new technologies can enhance the effectiveness of existing systems. Consider upgrading surveillance equipment, such as cameras and sensors, to models with higher resolution or advanced features like motion detection and facial recognition. Implementing smart technology, such as automated lighting and remote monitoring systems, can also increase security while offering convenience to residents. Regularly research and assess new technological solutions to ensure that the community remains at the forefront of security innovation.

Physical security measures, such as lighting, fencing, and locks, should also be periodically reviewed and updated. Ensure that all entry points to the community are secure and well-lit to deter potential intruders. Consider installing additional barriers or access control systems where necessary, particularly in vulnerable areas identified during the assessment. Simple upgrades, such as reinforced doors or shatterproof windows, can significantly enhance the physical security of homes and communal spaces.

Security plans must be adaptable to the evolving nature of threats. Develop a dynamic framework that allows for regular updates and revisions to protocols. This framework should outline clear procedures for identifying, assessing, and responding to new threats as they arise. Involve community members in the planning process to ensure that everyone understands their roles and responsibilities in maintaining security. By creating a proactive and inclusive security culture, residents become active participants in safeguarding their neighborhood.

Training and education play a crucial role in updating security measures. Offer workshops and seminars on topics such as situational awareness, emergency response, and personal safety. These events equip residents with the knowledge and skills needed to recognize and address potential security threats. Encourage ongoing learning and development by providing access to resources and information on the latest security trends and practices. A well-informed community is better prepared to adapt to changes and respond effectively to challenges.

Communication is key to maintaining an updated security strategy. Establish clear channels for sharing information about security updates, incidents, and best practices. Use a combination of digital platforms, such as community websites and social media, and traditional methods, like newsletters and bulletin boards, to reach all residents. Regularly communicate updates to security plans and encourage feedback to ensure that the community remains engaged and informed.

Collaboration with local law enforcement and security professionals can enhance the community's capacity to update and implement security measures. These partnerships provide access to expertise, resources, and support that can bolster the community's security efforts. Engage in joint training exercises, simulations, and information-sharing initiatives to strengthen relationships and improve coordination during emergencies. By working together, communities and law enforcement can develop a comprehensive and cohesive approach to security.

Regular testing and evaluation of security measures are essential to ensure their effectiveness. Conduct drills and simulations to assess the community's response to various scenarios, such as natural disasters, criminal activity, or health emergencies. These exercises provide valuable insights into the strengths and weaknesses of current plans, allowing for targeted updates and improvements. Involve residents in these activities to foster a sense of ownership and commitment to maintaining security.

# Learning from Real-World Experiences

When it comes to security, the wisdom drawn from real-world experiences is invaluable. These lessons, often etched in the aftermath of incidents, provide insights that can shape future strategies and help communities bolster their defenses. Learning from past experiences not only prepares us for future challenges but also fortifies our resilience, turning every encounter into an opportunity for growth and improvement.

To begin with, one of the most effective ways to learn from real-world experiences is through a thorough examination of past incidents. This involves understanding exactly what happened, why it occurred, and what could have been done to prevent it. Whether it's a natural disaster, an unexpected emergency, or a security breach, each incident holds valuable lessons. By analyzing these events, communities can identify vulnerabilities in their systems and processes, and develop strategies to mitigate future risks. This reflective practice turns every challenge into a learning opportunity, enhancing preparedness and response.

The first step in this process is to conduct a detailed analysis of past incidents. This involves collecting data and information on the event, understanding root causes, and assessing the effectiveness of the response. For instance, in the case of a natural disaster, understanding the sequence of events, how the community responded, and what could have been done differently can offer valuable insights. Similarly, in a security breach, identifying vulnerabilities, assessing the response, and understanding how the breach occurred can help prevent future incidents. By examining these factors, communities can develop strategies to prevent recurrence and mitigate risks.

Moreover, learning from real-world experiences is not limited to simply understanding what went wrong. It also involves celebrating successes, recognizing what went right, and building on strengths. By analyzing successful interventions, communities can identify best practices, highlight strengths, and implement effective strategies. This not only boosts confidence but also provides a roadmap for future responses. It is important to remember that even in challenging situations, there are valuable lessons to be learned, and successes to be celebrated.

Another critical aspect of learning from real-world experiences is the importance of continuous improvement. This involves continuously learning, adapting, and improving based on past experiences. Whether it's an emergency response, a security breach, or a natural disaster, each incident provides an opportunity to learn and improve. By continuously evaluating and reassessing strategies, communities can ensure that they are better prepared for future challenges. This may involve updating security measures, improving communication protocols, or enhancing response capabilities. By continuously learning and improving, communities can build resilience and be better prepared for future challenges.

One of the most effective ways to learn from real-world experiences is through collaboration and sharing of knowledge. This involves working together, sharing insights, and learning from each other. By fostering a culture of collaboration and knowledge sharing, communities can learn from each other's experiences, share best practices, and develop effective strategies. This not only enhances learning but also strengthens relationships and builds a sense of community. By working together, communities can learn from each other, share insights, and develop effective strategies.

The importance of learning from real-world experiences cannot be overstated. By understanding the lessons of the past, communities can build a culture of resilience, adaptability, and preparedness. This involves not only learning from past experiences but also celebrating successes, building on strengths, and continuously improving. By fostering a culture of learning, communities can build resilience, enhance preparedness, and be better equipped to face the challenges of the future.

## Continuously Improving Your Strategies

Continuous improvement is the backbone of resilience, especially in a world where threats and conditions evolve at an unprecedented pace. Communities need to adopt a mindset that embraces ongoing learning and adaptation to enhance their strategies effectively. By continuously refining their approaches, neighborhoods can stay ahead of potential challenges and maintain a safe and thriving environment.

The journey towards continuous improvement begins with a commitment to reflection and evaluation. After any incident or drill, it's crucial to assess the performance of existing strategies. This involves gathering feedback from all stakeholders, including residents, local authorities, and emergency services. Understanding their perspectives helps identify what worked well and what needs enhancement. This feedback loop not only pinpoints areas for improvement but also encourages community members to take an active role in shaping safety measures.

Data plays a significant role in informing strategy updates. By collecting and analyzing data related to incidents, response times, and outcomes, communities can identify patterns and trends. This data-driven approach allows for evidence-based decision-making, ensuring that updates are grounded in reality rather than speculation. Regularly reviewing crime statistics, environmental reports, and health data can provide valuable insights into emerging threats and help prioritize areas that require attention.

Another essential aspect of continuous improvement is staying informed about advancements in technology and best practices. The field of security and disaster management is ever-evolving, with new tools and techniques emerging regularly. Communities should make it a priority to stay abreast of these developments, attending workshops and conferences, and engaging with experts in the field. By integrating cutting-edge technology and innovative practices, neighborhoods can enhance their preparedness and response capabilities.

Training and education are pivotal in ensuring that community members are equipped to handle evolving threats. Regular training sessions should be organized to update residents on new procedures, tools, and techniques. These sessions can cover a range of topics, from first aid and emergency response to cybersecurity and personal safety. Encouraging continuous learning not only builds individual competencies but also fosters a culture of resilience and adaptability within the community.

Partnerships and collaboration with external organizations can significantly enhance a community's ability to improve its strategies continuously. By working with local governments, non-profits, and neighboring communities, neighborhoods can share resources, knowledge, and expertise. These partnerships can facilitate joint training exercises, simulations, and information-sharing initiatives, ensuring that all parties are aligned and working towards common goals. Collaboration also opens the door to accessing additional resources and support, which can be invaluable in implementing strategy updates.

Flexibility and adaptability are key traits for any community seeking to continuously improve its strategies. Plans and measures should be dynamic, allowing for adjustments as new information becomes available or conditions change. This requires a willingness to revisit and revise strategies regularly, keeping them relevant and effective. By fostering a mindset of adaptability, communities can navigate uncertainties with confidence and agility.

Celebrating successes and acknowledging progress is an often-overlooked aspect of continuous improvement. Recognizing the efforts of individuals and groups who contribute to enhancing community strategies reinforces the value of ongoing development. Whether through public recognition, awards, or community events, celebrating achievements motivates residents to remain engaged and committed to the process. This positive reinforcement helps maintain momentum and encourages further participation in future initiatives.

# Preparing for Future Challenges

Anticipating future challenges and preparing to face them is a crucial aspect of any community's strategy for resilience. In an ever-changing world, the ability to foresee potential threats and develop robust plans can make a significant difference in a neighborhood's capacity to withstand disruptions.

The foundation of any effective preparation strategy lies in understanding the potential challenges that a community may face. This begins with a thorough risk assessment, identifying possible threats such as natural disasters, economic shifts, technological changes, and social dynamics. Consider the geographical location, historical data, and emerging trends to create a comprehensive profile of risks. Engaging with experts, local authorities, and community members can provide diverse perspectives and enhance the accuracy of this assessment.

Once potential challenges are identified, the next step is to prioritize them based on their likelihood and potential impact. Not all threats will pose the same level of risk, and resources should be allocated accordingly. By categorizing risks into high, medium, and low priorities, communities can focus their efforts on areas that require immediate attention while keeping an eye on less urgent concerns. This prioritization ensures that plans are both strategic and resource-efficient.

Developing a comprehensive preparedness plan is essential for addressing future challenges. This plan should outline specific actions to be taken in response to each identified threat, detailing roles and responsibilities, communication protocols, and resource allocation. Involving community members in the planning process ensures that the plan is practical and considers the unique needs and capabilities of the neighborhood. A well-crafted plan serves as a roadmap, guiding the community through potential crises with clarity and confidence.

Flexibility is a key component of any preparedness plan. As conditions evolve, so too should the strategies designed to address them. Regularly reviewing and updating plans ensures they remain relevant and effective. This dynamic approach allows for the incorporation of new information, technologies, and lessons learned from past experiences. By maintaining flexibility, communities can adapt to changing circumstances and remain resilient in the face of unforeseen challenges.

Education and training are vital in preparing for future challenges. Providing residents with the knowledge and skills they need to respond effectively to potential threats empowers them to take proactive measures. Workshops, drills, and simulations can cover a range of topics, from emergency response and first aid to cybersecurity and environmental awareness. By fostering a culture of continuous learning, communities build a collective capacity to navigate challenges with confidence and competence.

Collaboration with external partners can greatly enhance a community's preparedness efforts. Establishing relationships with local governments, non-profits, and neighboring communities facilitates the sharing of resources, knowledge, and expertise. Joint training exercises and information-sharing initiatives can improve coordination and strengthen collective resilience. These partnerships can also provide access to additional support and resources during times of crisis, enhancing the community's ability to respond effectively.

Communication is a critical element in preparing for future challenges. Establishing clear and effective communication channels ensures that all residents are informed and engaged. Regular updates on preparedness efforts, potential threats, and community initiatives keep everyone in the loop. Encouraging feedback and input from residents fosters a sense of ownership and participation, strengthening the community's commitment to preparedness.

Innovation and technology play a significant role in enhancing preparedness efforts. Leveraging advancements in technology can provide communities with valuable tools for monitoring, predicting, and responding to potential threats. From early warning systems and data analytics to communication platforms and resource management tools, technology offers a range of solutions that can enhance a community's capacity to prepare for and respond to challenges. Staying informed about technological advancements and integrating them into preparedness efforts can provide a significant advantage in navigating future uncertainties.

Celebrating progress and milestones is an important aspect of maintaining momentum in preparedness efforts. Recognizing the achievements of individuals and groups who contribute to the community's resilience reinforces the value of proactive measures and encourages continued participation. Celebrations can take the form of community events, awards, or public acknowledgments, highlighting the collective efforts and successes of the neighborhood.

# CONCLUSION

# ACHIEVING UNBREAKABLE SECURITY AND PEACE OF MIND

## Reviewing Your Preparedness Journey

Reflecting on the journey toward achieving unbreakable security and peace of mind is as crucial as the steps taken along the way. It is in this reflection that communities can truly understand the depths of their preparedness, learning from past experiences and reinforcing their future strategies. This chapter serves as a guide to review and assess the efforts that have been made, ensuring that the path forward is as strong and resilient as possible.

The first step in reviewing your preparedness journey is to conduct a comprehensive audit of the measures that have been implemented. This involves taking a detailed look at the strategies, protocols, and systems that have been put in place over time. Identify what has been successful and what may need further refinement. Consider factors such as the effectiveness of communication channels, the reliability of technology and infrastructure, and the strength of community engagement. By examining these elements, neighborhoods can gain a clear picture of their current preparedness level and identify areas for improvement.

Community feedback is an invaluable resource in this review process. Engaging with residents, local authorities, and other stakeholders provides diverse perspectives and insights into how well strategies are working. Organize community meetings or surveys to gather input on various aspects of preparedness, including response times, communication effectiveness, and overall satisfaction with the measures in place. This collaborative approach not only highlights areas of success but also uncovers potential gaps that may have been overlooked.

One of the most important aspects of reviewing your preparedness journey is to celebrate the milestones and achievements that have been reached along the way. Recognizing the hard work and dedication of individuals and groups who have contributed to the community's resilience reinforces the value of these efforts. Whether through public acknowledgments, awards, or community events, celebrating successes boosts morale and encourages continued participation in future initiatives. It serves as a reminder of what has been accomplished and motivates everyone to keep striving for improvement.

Reflecting on past incidents and responses is another crucial component of the review process. Analyzing how the community has handled previous challenges provides valuable lessons and insights that can inform future strategies. Consider what went well and what could have been done differently, and incorporate these lessons into future plans. By learning from past experiences, communities build a stronger foundation for resilience and adaptability, ensuring they are better prepared for whatever comes next.

Flexibility and adaptability are essential traits in the ongoing pursuit of unbreakable security and peace of mind. As conditions and threats evolve, so too should the strategies designed to address them. Regularly revisiting and updating plans ensures they remain relevant and effective. This adaptive approach allows for the incorporation of new information, technologies, and best practices, keeping the community at the forefront of preparedness. By maintaining flexibility, neighborhoods can confidently navigate uncertainties and continue to thrive.

Collaboration with external partners remains a vital part of the preparedness journey. Strengthening relationships with local governments, non-profits, and other communities enhances the sharing of resources, knowledge, and expertise. These partnerships provide additional support and resources during times of crisis and contribute to a collective approach to resilience. By working together, communities can tackle challenges more effectively and build a network of support that extends beyond their immediate borders.

Innovation plays a pivotal role in achieving unbreakable security. Staying informed about technological advancements and integrating them into preparedness efforts can provide significant advantages. From early warning systems and communication platforms to data analytics and resource management tools, technology offers a range of solutions that enhance the community's capacity to prepare for and respond to challenges. By embracing innovation, neighborhoods can remain agile and responsive to the ever-changing landscape of threats.

Ultimately, reviewing your preparedness journey is about more than just assessing past efforts; it's about charting a course for the future. By understanding the progress that has been made, celebrating successes, and identifying areas for improvement, communities can continue to build resilience and enhance their security. This reflection provides a roadmap for the path forward, ensuring that neighborhoods remain safe, connected, and prepared for whatever the future may hold.

As we conclude this chapter, it is clear that the journey toward unbreakable security and peace of mind is ongoing. It requires dedication, collaboration, and a commitment to continuous improvement. By embracing these principles and remaining vigilant in the face of evolving threats, communities can achieve a level of preparedness that ensures the safety and well-being of all residents. This pursuit of resilience not only safeguards the present but also creates a legacy of security and peace for generations to come.

## Sustaining Long-Term Security and Resilience

Sustaining long-term security and resilience is a multifaceted endeavor that demands unwavering commitment, strategic foresight, and a community-driven approach. As we wrap up the exploration of building unbreakable security, it becomes apparent that the journey is continuous, evolving with the challenges it seeks to guard against. Embracing this dynamic nature is key to ensuring that neighborhoods not only thrive but also stand resilient in the face of adversity.

At the heart of sustaining security is the commitment to ongoing assessment and evolution of strategies. The landscape of threats is ever-changing, influenced by technological advancements, societal shifts, and environmental changes. Communities must remain vigilant, regularly reassessing their security measures and protocols to address new vulnerabilities. This begins with a thorough audit of existing systems, evaluating their effectiveness, and identifying areas for enhancement. Such evaluations must be data-driven, harnessing information from past incidents, expert advice, and community feedback to inform future strategies. This iterative process ensures that plans remain relevant and robust, capable of adapting to emerging challenges.

Engagement and collaboration within the community play a pivotal role in maintaining long-term security. Security is not a solitary pursuit; it is a collective responsibility that thrives on the active participation of all members. Encouraging residents to take ownership of their role in community safety fosters a sense of responsibility and commitment. Organizing regular forums, workshops, and training sessions creates opportunities for residents to engage, learn, and contribute to the community's resilience. These interactions build trust and solidarity, reinforcing the notion that security is a shared endeavor.

Building strong partnerships beyond the community's borders is equally essential. Collaborating with local governments, law enforcement agencies, non-profit organizations, and neighboring communities can amplify the resources and expertise available. These partnerships facilitate the sharing of best practices, joint training exercises, and coordinated responses in times of crisis. By leveraging external support, communities can enhance their preparedness and response capabilities, ensuring a comprehensive approach to security.

Innovation and technology are indispensable tools in the quest for sustainable security. The rapid pace of technological advancement offers communities a wealth of opportunities to enhance their security infrastructure. From integrating smart surveillance systems and data analytics to deploying early warning systems and communication platforms, technology can significantly bolster a community's resilience. Staying informed about technological trends and incorporating them into security strategies ensures that communities remain agile and responsive to potential threats.

Education and continuous learning are foundational to sustaining security. Empowering residents with the knowledge and skills they need to navigate potential challenges builds a culture of preparedness. Offering regular training sessions, workshops, and educational resources keeps residents informed and equipped to respond effectively to various scenarios. Encouraging a mindset of lifelong learning fosters adaptability and resilience, ensuring that the community can navigate uncertainties with confidence.

A proactive and adaptable mindset is crucial for sustaining security over the long term. This requires not only responding to threats as they arise but also anticipating future challenges and preparing accordingly. Scenario planning, simulations, and risk assessments enable communities to explore potential threats and develop strategies to mitigate them. By thinking ahead and planning for diverse eventualities, neighborhoods can build flexibility into their security plans, ensuring they are prepared for whatever may come.

# Celebrating Your Achievements

Celebrating achievements is more than a momentary acknowledgment; it's a powerful recognition of the collective effort, resilience, and commitment that has propelled a community towards unbreakable security and peace of mind. This celebration marks not just the milestones achieved but also the journey traveled, highlighting the unwavering dedication of every individual involved. By celebrating, communities foster a sense of pride and unity, reinforcing the values that underpin their strength and solidarity.

A key aspect of celebrating achievements lies in recognizing the contributions of all members within the community. Security and resilience are built on the efforts of many, from local leaders and emergency responders to volunteers and residents who have committed to collective safety. Acknowledging these contributions can take many forms—public accolades, awards ceremonies, or community gatherings. Each recognition serves as a testament to the hard work and perseverance that has been invested in building a safer environment.

To truly appreciate the progress made, it's essential to reflect on the challenges overcome along the way. Every obstacle faced and surmounted provides a learning opportunity, underscoring the resilience and adaptability of the community. Whether it's successfully implementing new safety protocols, effectively responding to a crisis, or fostering greater community engagement, each challenge conquered strengthens the community's foundation. Reflecting on these successes reinforces the capability and resourcefulness that drive ongoing efforts.

Celebrations also provide an opportunity to share stories of triumph and inspiration that have emerged throughout the journey. Personal narratives and testimonials from community members can illuminate the impact of collective efforts, creating a tapestry of experiences that capture the essence of the community's journey. These stories not only inspire others but also serve as a reminder of the bonds and relationships that have been forged in pursuit of a common goal.

Engaging the broader community in celebrations is crucial for reinforcing a sense of belonging and participation. Organizing events that bring people together fosters camaraderie and strengthens the social fabric that underpins security and resilience. Community festivals, open days at local emergency services, or collaborative workshops can provide platforms for interaction, learning, and enjoyment. Such events highlight the importance of collective action and remind everyone that security is a shared responsibility.

Looking back on the achievements, it's important to recognize the role of innovation and creativity in reaching these milestones. Embracing new technologies, exploring alternative solutions, and thinking outside the box have often been pivotal in overcoming challenges. Celebrating these innovative approaches encourages a culture of creativity and adaptability, ensuring that the community remains agile and responsive to future threats. This acknowledgment of ingenuity fosters an environment where new ideas are welcomed and explored.

# Planning for Ongoing Improvement

As we reach the conclusion of our journey toward unbreakable security and peace of mind, the importance of planning for ongoing improvement becomes ever more apparent. In a world where threats continually evolve, stagnation is not an option. The true hallmark of a resilient community lies in its ability to adapt and enhance its strategies over time, remaining vigilant and prepared for whatever the future may hold.

Ongoing improvement begins with a commitment to constant evaluation and reflection. Regularly assessing the effectiveness of current strategies is crucial. This involves analyzing how well systems have performed, identifying any weaknesses, and exploring potential enhancements. By maintaining a culture of continuous evaluation, communities ensure that their security measures evolve in line with emerging challenges and technological advancements. This process requires meticulous documentation of incidents and responses, which serves as a valuable repository of lessons learned and informs future strategies.

Open communication channels within the community are essential for fostering improvement. Encouraging feedback from all stakeholders, including residents, businesses, local authorities, and emergency services, provides diverse perspectives that can illuminate blind spots and inform enhancements. This dialogue should be ongoing, creating a feedback loop that continually feeds into the community's strategy development. Regular forums, surveys, and town hall meetings can serve as platforms for this exchange, ensuring that all voices are heard and considered.

Innovation plays a pivotal role in planning for ongoing improvement. Embracing new technologies and methodologies can significantly enhance a community's capacity to respond to threats. From advanced surveillance systems and data analytics to improved communication platforms and resource management tools, technology offers a multitude of solutions that can be leveraged to strengthen resilience. Staying abreast of technological trends and integrating them into security strategies ensures that communities remain agile and responsive to the ever-changing landscape of threats.

Education and training are indispensable components of any improvement plan. Providing residents with the knowledge and skills they need to address potential challenges empowers them to act confidently and effectively. Regular training sessions, workshops, and simulations keep the community informed and prepared, fostering a culture of resilience. Encouraging lifelong learning and skill development ensures that community members remain adaptable and capable of navigating uncertainties with competence.

Collaboration with external partners enhances a community's capacity for ongoing improvement. Establishing strong relationships with local governments, non-profits, academic institutions, and neighboring communities facilitates the sharing of resources, knowledge, and best practices. These partnerships can lead to joint training exercises, coordinated responses, and collaborative initiatives that strengthen the community's overall resilience. By tapping into external expertise, neighborhoods can access additional support and resources that bolster their ongoing improvement efforts.

Flexibility and adaptability are key attributes for any community committed to ongoing improvement. Plans and strategies should be dynamic, allowing for adjustments as new information becomes available or conditions change. This requires a willingness to revisit and revise strategies regularly, ensuring they remain relevant and effective. By fostering a mindset of adaptability, communities can navigate uncertainties with confidence and agility, maintaining their trajectory toward unbreakable security and peace of mind.

# Final Thoughts on Home Security and Peace

Achieving unbreakable security and peace of mind in our homes is not merely about installing the latest gadgets or implementing a checklist of measures. It is a living, breathing process, one that integrates thoughtful planning, continuous adaptation, and a proactive mindset. As we wrap up this exploration, the focus shifts to the lasting impressions and broader strategies that ensure our homes remain sanctuaries of safety and serenity.

Home security begins with understanding the unique needs and vulnerabilities of your household. Each home is different, and so are its security requirements. This understanding starts with a thorough assessment of potential risks—both external and internal. Consider the geographical features, the community dynamics, and even the daily routines of household members. This comprehensive evaluation helps in tailoring security measures that are specific and effective, rather than generic and potentially inadequate.

Once you have a clear picture of the security landscape, the next step is to implement a layered approach. Think of security as an onion, with multiple layers that an intruder must peel away to gain access. This includes physical barriers such as locks, gates, and surveillance systems, but also extends to digital security measures like firewalls and encryption for your smart devices. Each layer serves as an additional hurdle for potential threats, collectively creating a robust shield for your home.

However, technology alone cannot guarantee peace of mind. The human element is crucial. Training and awareness are vital components of any security strategy. Ensure that every member of the household understands the importance of security measures and knows how to use them effectively. Regularly review emergency procedures and conduct drills to ensure that everyone is prepared in the event of a security breach. Knowledge empowers individuals to act swiftly and confidently, reducing panic and enhancing safety.

Community engagement is another vital aspect of home security. A well-connected neighborhood is a safer one. Establishing strong relationships with neighbors can create a network of mutual vigilance and support. Neighborhood watch programs, community meetings, and social media groups can enhance communication and collective awareness, allowing for swift action in the event of suspicious activity. When people look out for one another, the entire community benefits from increased security and peace of mind.

Adaptability is key in maintaining long-term security. As threats evolve, so too must your strategies. Regularly updating security systems, incorporating new technologies, and staying informed about the latest security trends are essential. This proactive approach ensures that your home remains a step ahead of potential threats. It also involves being open to feedback and learning from past experiences, continuously refining your approach to security.

Celebrating small victories and milestones is an often-overlooked aspect of security planning. Every successful deterrent, every thwarted attempt, and every peaceful night is a testament to the effectiveness of your security measures. Acknowledging these successes boosts morale and reinforces the value of ongoing vigilance and improvement. It also serves as a reminder of the collective effort required to maintain a secure environment.

In the pursuit of unbreakable security, it is essential to balance vigilance with a sense of peace. Security measures should not create an atmosphere of fear or paranoia. Instead, they should foster confidence and reassurance, allowing you to live comfortably and freely. This balance is achieved through thoughtful planning, consistent communication, and a commitment to fostering a positive and secure environment.

Ultimately, the journey to achieving unbreakable security and peace of mind is a continuous one. It requires dedication, adaptability, and a willingness to learn and grow. By embracing these principles, you create a home that is not only safe but also a haven of tranquility. As we conclude this exploration, the path forward is clear: stay informed, stay connected, and stay committed to the ongoing pursuit of security and peace. In doing so, you ensure that your home remains a sanctuary—a place where safety and serenity reign supreme.

# EXTRA CONTENTS

## Ebook On Survival Without Electricity

This ebook offers essential strategies to help you thrive during power outages. Discover practical tips and expert advice on staying prepared, ensuring that you and your family can maintain safety and comfort without relying on electricity.

## Ebook On How To Purify Water

Clean water is critical for survival. In this bonus ebook, you'll learn Navy SEAL-level techniques to purify water in any situation, ensuring you have access to safe drinking water no matter the circumstances.

## Audiobook

Whether you're on the go or multitasking, the audiobook version of *Navy SEAL-Proof Your Home* ensures you won't miss any of the life-saving strategies. Listen to expert advice and actionable steps for fortifying your home while maximizing your time.

## Checklist Printable First Aid Kit

Stay organized and ready with this printable first aid kit checklist. This handy guide helps you assemble all the vital supplies you need to handle emergencies with confidence, ensuring peace of mind for you and your family.

Scan the QR CODE or click on the link below and access the bonuses

https://navyseals.dsinternationalagency.com/first-page-8271-4116-8940

Made in United States
Troutdale, OR
12/24/2024